Adjustment
in Intercultural Marriage

Adjustment
in Intercultural Marriage

Edited by:
Wen-Shing Tseng
John F. McDermott, Jr.
Thomas W. Maretzki

Associate Editor:
Gardiner Jones

Department of Psychiatry
John A. Burns School of Medicine
University of Hawaii

Distributed by The University Press of Hawaii
2840 Kolowalu Street, Honolulu, Hawaii 96822

The responsibility for the content and editorial preparation of this book rests with the Department of Psychiatry, University of Hawaii.

Manufactured in the United States of America

ISBN 0-8248-0579-8

Contents

Preface

This book will go to press about ten years after we admitted the first class of medical students to the University of Hawaii School of Medicine. If I had been asked, at that time, to describe the kinds of scholarly activities I would hope for our faculty to be conducting in 1977, a ghostly shadow of this book would have come to my mind. This is not simply on the basis that our faculty have indeed made use of the limitless resources of Hawaii as a psychosocial laboratory, or that they have displayed a disciplined scientific curiosity about our unique society (or even that they made that incredible activaticn jump from concept to publication). In those early days we hoped for a warm, humanistic medical school worthy of the people of Hawaii. I am, therefore, deeply gratified that through this collection of essays there runs a current of humanism and concern that is exactly what we would have hoped for from our Department of Psychiatry. Incredibly, it seems to be working.

In most cultures, marriage and the subsequent rearing of children is the most important set of events of adult life. Since that young parent's childhood is usually passed in the milieu of his or her own parents' marriage, it follows that marriage (our parents plus our own) is a lifelong experience of overwhelming importance for most of humankind. One of my observations, as an administrator, is that most people pay fanatic attention to controlling trivia (parking, distilled water supply, etc.) and allow matters such as health and marriage to simply happen to them at the whim of a generally indifferent (if not hostile) universe. My simplistic partial explanation of this is that the most important areas of our lives are governed by very large assumptions—assumptions so large that we have no conception that they *are* assumptions. A challenge to one of those assumptions, as from a person of another culture, is perceived as a challenge to common sense, Holy Writ, or grandmother.

Televised football has introduced some new stresses into the American home, and mildly humorous conflict arises because of the differences in basic assumptions about the importance of football between men and women raised in the *same* culture. An extrapolation of this to the conflict of unacknowledged but different assumptions about sex roles, child rearing, and the whole warp and woof of married life gives a glimpse of the scale of problems presenting in an intercultural marriage. At the same time the interweaving of totally different threads in the warp and woof can lead to strange and lovely patterns, with a richness that outweighs the hazards of unrecognized clashes.

Intercultural marriages are the societal norm in Hawaii and most people embarking on such marriages are not only aware that a lot of give and take will be necessary, but also they usually have in common a strong underpinning of that curious "intercultural culture" that is characteristic of Hawaii. On a one-to-one basis, the basic love and considerateness of a healthy marriage is enhanced by society's comfortable acceptance and enfolding of cultural idiosyncracies. As is developed in more detail in this book, however, the more recalcitrant problems arise when child rearing begins, perhaps because the assumptions of each parent (and especially the grandparent) are so large that conciliatory compromises seem to fly in the face of nature and common sense. When, as is often the case, an intercultural marriage involves one or more spouse who has not been brought up in the Hawaiian intercultural culture, then the adjustment problems are even greater. Nevertheless, a very large proportion of Hawaii's citizens are derived from such unions, and we are undoubtedly the most peacefully integrated intercultural society in the world. Therefore, for all the potential problems, the intercultural families in Hawaii are doing some things right, and perhaps the rest of the world can learn from them.

A character in Japanese fiction was much frustrated by a Zen Koan: "What was your true face prior to the birth of your parents?" This book provides no answers that would satisfy the fictional Zen master, but perhaps the question itself describes the theme my colleagues have so boldly addressed.

Terence A. Rogers, Ph.D.
Dean, John A. Burns School of Medicine
University of Hawaii

Introduction

This is the second volume in a cross-cultural series produced by the Department of Psychiatry. Our first work, *People and Cultures in Hawaii*, examined each culture in Hawaii and the development of its own historical identity. The special focus was on the individual dimension of human functioning which bridges these cultures and is the carrier of cultural inheritance.

The ways in which individual cultures intermingle with the resultant development of new cultural systems or subsystems have been relatively neglected. Thus, the subject of this book is intercultural marriage which provides a unique model for the intense study of adjustment between cultures and focuses on the family as the carrier of culture. We examine the processes by which marriage partners from different cultures synthesize their individual values and attitudes and then convey a *new* cultural inheritance to their children. A husband and wife bring to their marriage their own particular personalities and combine to form a new mutual system in which each becomes a part of the self-system of the other. Once this has happened, much of the growth which forms an enduring relationship develops through parenthood. Yet, in intercultural marriages, the conscious synthesis between marriage partners may be temporarily lost with the arrival of children. A second and deeper layer of beliefs and values based on the individuals' own earlier childhood experiences when culture made its unconscious indelible imprint may emerge. Thus, the result may be either synthesis or conflict.

We are in a period of transition in the United States. Until recently, intercultural marriages were viewed negatively or with suspicion by our society. Most of the studies of intercultural marriages have of necessity emphasized the political, social and psychological problems which have occurred in America over the past several decades. In Hawaii, however, there exist so many cultural groups that multiple examples of intercultural marriage among groups who have lived side by side for generations can readily be seen and observed. Indeed, the early New England immigrants soon intermarried with the native Hawaiians. This is the reason why it is often said that the early breakdown of the "last taboo", that cultural intermarriage, set the tone for Hawaii's place as a unique laboratory where cultures live together and can be studied. Today, more than 50 percent of current marriage in Hawaii are intercultural, and thus they have become the statistical norm in a society which sees such combinations with relatively less preexisting prejudice than the rest of the United States.

The editors are much indebted and will long remain grateful to those who helped make this book possible. Our special thanks to Dean Terence A. Rogers for his support and example. To the families who have taught us so much, we are extremely indebted. The teamwork which so characterizes the efforts of the members of the Department of Psychiatry of the John A. Burns School of Medicine in teaching and research is evident in this book. While the editors are responsible for the overall organization and flow from one chapter to another, each chapter and the relationships between them is the work of the members of the faculty. The chapters are based largely on the clinical experience of these experts who work every day with our multi-ethnic, intercultural population. In order to illustrate certain points, some stereotypic examples are used. We hope that the reader understands the necessity of considering individual variations so that such stereotypes are viewed in a relative rather than a literal fashion. For example, although we speak of culture rather than ethnicity, or race, it is notoriously difficult to identify specific cultural groups accurately. Therefore, certain ethnic and racial groups are often identified for the purpose of illustration alone.

The opening chapters of the book deal with the general and universal aspects of marriage and mate selection, then move to motivations for intercultural marriage. Problem areas and adjustment patterns in intercultural marriage, with particular reference to childrearing and family interaction, are then considered in detail. A special aspect, the clinical study of intercultural marriages under the stress of chronic illness is also considered. Finally, a concluding chapter offers suggestions for counseling intercultural marriages. However, it should be kept in mind that the editors and authors firmly believe that prevention is the best cure. Understanding and awareness of different cultural patterns can help to anticipate potential problems from the clash of values and attitudes. Prevention can keep them from becoming disruptive, and provide the partners with more options toward early resolution. Success is seen when each of the members, in relationship with one another, achieves a new level of personality integration and maturation and the family unit progresses in its development.

Having been encouraged by the response to our first volume, *People and Cultures in Hawaii,* we hope that this one and subsequent others will extract the most significant aspects of culture and examine them in their various forms, combining breadth and depth with attempts toward synthesis rather than narrowness or polarity of point of view. Indeed, in the field of culture and human funtioning, where so much remains unknown, the appropriate function of our series is as much to raise questions as to answer them, as much to focus on or clarify issues as to resolve them. Culture itself, which is the concern of our series, is a very complex phenomenon. Everyone belongs to a culture; many teach and write about it, but no one has yet completely defined it!

John F. McDermott, Jr., M.D.
Chairman, Department of Psychiatry
John A. Burns School of Medicine
University of Hawaii

1

Intercultural Marriage: An Introduction

Thomas W. Maretzki, Ph.D.

This book is about intercultural marriage which in Hawaii and in other places is rapidly increasing. By intercultural marriage, we mean the marriage which takes place between spouses of different cultural backgrounds. They may be different in their values, beliefs, customs, traditions or style of life so that cultural dimensions are a relatively significant aspect of such marriages. By focusing on this type of marriage, the authors suggest that it is unconventional and, therefore, implies some risks. In this introduction, we will attempt a perspective for the remainder of the book by providing background information and some speculative thoughts.

Since the authors vary in their interpretations, we may assume that the reader, too, is not clear about the meaning of the term intercultural marriage. Taking a specific married couple as an example, how can one be sure whether or not their marriage is intercultural? If intercultural marriage is not conventional, it is deviant? If deviant, are there risks in such a marriage for which preventive and interventive clinical approaches have been developed? The presentations in the chapters of this book should provide some answers and stimulate others to think further about the subject.

To what extent intercultural marriage merits separate treatment from marriage in general becomes significant when clinical situations point to specific problems arising among such unions, and when practical answers are sought by various professionals. The orientation of this book—

its presentation of background and documentary materials uses both scholarly and clinical knowledge and experiences.

The search for an appropriate definition of intercultural marriage leads to the related concept of interracial marriage. In a recent book on this subject, the authors seem to assume that anyone can tell when race is involved so that there is no doubt whether or not a marriage is interracial. Their emphasis is primarily on marriage between blacks and whites.

Race in the minds of people is real enough. In popular usage and application of widely held beliefs that specific physical traits are common to a race, the assignment of an individual to a racial group is determined by appearance. Fundamental to racial distinctions is the common concern with ancestry and with relative values given to one's own ancestry when compared with others. It is irrelevant to the popular opinion and usage of racial distinctions that from a scientific point of view race cannot be established loosely in observable physical characteristics, but is a biological term referring to the assortment of physiochemical hereditary elements in the invisible cell structure of each individual. A basis for the popular concepts of race is the significance of ancestry and culture, the combination of factors which in recent years have entered popular usage through the term "ethnicity".

Intercultural marriage is broader and more descriptive as a term of the range of phenomena which make certain unions between two persons a special focus of interest. Between blacks and whites, there are usually significant cultural differences, but that is also true for Chinese and Japanese who, according to widely held views, belong to the same race. Although the meanings of race and culture are vague, the use of these terms creates social realities. Race as a social concept and culture as experienced through contacts with others are important elements in the identity of the individual. When two persons enter into marriage, their relationship over an extended period of time will be very much influenced by communications between the two, and by the kind of identity each partner holds, and is able to merge harmoniously with that of the other. The involvement includes children, parents and other people of importance to one or both partners.

Culture in one of its simplest meanings refers to the widely shared customs or traditions of a relatively homogeneous population. In such a social entity, marriage is arranged according to customs which specify eligible partners, ways of bringing about marriage, and behaviors and relationships appropriate for marriage. Presumably all marriages in such social groups are intracultural. The anthropological literature is abundant with examples of culturally homogeneous tribal societies or small peasant communities where there are, or at least were, few population

2

movements and few contacts with outsiders. Such societies are bound by traditions and rules which affect all individuals and leave little room for individual expression contrary to the conventional. As these societies change or tend to disappear, the customary types of marriage also diminish. Intercultural marriages, we suggest here, are the extreme contrasts with these vanishing traditional marriages. It is, of course, also known that anthropologists often construct "ideal models" of marriage types which even in stable and isolated societies are subject to occasional exceptions of established customs.

We need not even go to the unfamiliar and culturally distant societies. Close to the home of American readers, we can point to tightly knit contemporary groups such as the Hutterites or Amish where marriage with persons of similar cultural background is not only a societal ideal, but carefully fostered and maintained. A clear awareness of the consequences for individuals and society, of a marriage with outsiders, regulates the behavior of adults and implies personal consequences if disobeyed.

Even though populations no longer live in cultural isolation, distinct cultural conventions regulate the way people do things in all aspects of their lives. Culture continues to be a factor in people's world view, how they conceptualize other persons and events, and how values and meanings are assigned. Culture as a characteristic of human groups continues even though cultural boundaries are much less distinct in modern societies and cultural forms change in some respects more rapidly. Constant changes and mutual influences bring about rather diverse patterns of culture like a mosaic that continuously changes its composition and colors. For people who live in Hawaii—even for those who have been in the islands only a short while—this idea of a blend of customs is quite familiar. There are many places with mixed cultures, but few with relatively open and conflict-free living situations as exist in Hawaii.

Entering and sustaining a marriage deeply involves human behavior. What is the function of culture in relation to human behavior? Culture provides rules of conduct for interpersonal relations. Seen from this perspective culture can be thought of as a grammar or calculus according to which married partners regulate their behavior toward each other, as parents with their children, as relatives with their own parents, with parents of the spouse, as well as with others related to them.

At some time in the evolution of man, marriage replaced the simpler relationships and functions of animal mating and care for the young. Behavior which in primates is considerably controlled by the interplay of dominance and submission between males and females in humans becomes subject to complex and abstract rules. The capacity for living by abstract rules is dependent on the mental ability for complex symbolization and its corollary, human language. How marriage developed for early man is beyond historical verification. The existing forms of marriage make it evident that no one particular form of marriage is typically human or natural. Rather, by taking a cross-cultural perspective we can see the significance of kinship in governing relationships between people. Marriage is regulated by kinship considerations in traditional societies. In those populations, marriage is more than just a union between two individuals. It involves groups of people in quite complicated systems of exchange of kin members in which the loss of one female, or one male, to another group is quite carefully calculated and needs to be recognized in reciprocal fashion either by a similar marriage which reestablishes the balance, or with the aid of an exchange of goods or services to compensate a kin group for the loss of a member.

If basic rules governed marriage in man's past, this is less true as traditional societies vanish. In the past, marriage partners could anticipate appropriate ways of behaving in marriage. Even if some traditional societies did not prepare individuals by abstracting and communicating important rules for behavior in advance, at least rules could be learned upon entering marriage because there were rules and they were relatively clear. If people were inadequately prepared, the necessary social support as well as sanctions helped to develop appropriate behavior. This is different in societies or in individual situations where there are neither preparations nor specific rules governing behavior. In those cases, the marriage partners have to develop their own arrangements.

We may wonder why people behave as they do, and why conformity with conventions can be found even if there are no severe punishments for infractions. Everyone has a theory about why people act the way they do, and why some behave contrary to expectations or customs by disregarding rules for behavior. Scholarly arguments on these issues remain inconclusive. A variety of forces, singly or in concert, are considered "sources" of behavior. Actually, these are only abstractions in the minds of people expressed as concepts which are then cited as motivators or inhibitors. Quite broadly, these forces are psychological or social, or a combination of both. Those explaining behavior which are thought to be part of the organism and presumably part of the hereditary system, are called human nature or instinct. Those which are a function of membership in a specific social group are referred to as customs or culture.

Since this discussion deals with mate selection and marriage, we can examine these forces and how they relate to cultural rules by using incest as an example. Incest refers to violations of restrictions on mating with very close relatives: parents and siblings in all societies, these and certain

4

categories of cousins in most societies. Incest prohibitions, therefore, concern marriage choices which are the very opposite of intercultural marriage. Restrictions on mating with close relatives do not yield to cultural changes and weakening of traditions. Strict social and legal sanctions cover violations of incest rules even though there is a great deal of evidence that it is a common and widespread practice of many people to have sexual relations with a forbidden relative. No forces of similar strength act on intercultural marriages.

Popular reasoning about restrictions of incest may invoke human nature as an explanatory principle. Human nature implies a behavioral tendency built into the organism in such a way that regardless of cultural background it will be found in humans. Noncultural forces in humans are referred to as biological and are found at the level of behavior that is shared with other animals, for example, in avoidance of situations dangerous to the organism, or essential to the survival of the organism. If incest were governed by human nature, or by biological forces built into the organism, then no rules regulating incest would be needed. The frequent sexual activities which violate incest rules are evidence against biological or innate traits. Instead, they point to the significance of culturally specified rules; although widespread, these may be disobeyed. Apparently, unions with persons close to oneself require extremely powerful regulators which, in their effects at least, are on a level with biological forces.

Freud's theory which claims an unconscious desire for sexual relations between closest relatives, mother and son, father and daughter, or siblings, explains the need for stringent cultural rules (often called incest taboos) as well as for their violation. Other social theorists have offered a different explanation for the universal avoidance of incest by invoking the principle of "familiarity breeds contempt." In this explanation, forces constraining incest would reflect aversion instead of unconscious desire. General sociological or social forces theory takes still another position in explaining the universal practice of marrying outside the group of closest relatives (family exogamy) by arguing that society would not function if close relatives marry. There are also genetic explanations which point to the risks involved in passing on undesirable recessive genes to offsprings by mating with close relatives who may be carriers of the same harmful hereditary traits, but these would elevate very recent and complicated scientific arguments to socially regulated behavior.

Although not subject to feelings, associations, and sanctions as drastic as those concerning incest prohibitions, the mating between members of different social groups has some parallels. These—as has been shown—are quite strong if "race" is a factor. One powerful psychological influence which has been suggested for racial separation is fear of pollution. This has been laid to specific psychological dynamics in some populations, ultimately anchored in human reactions to which such fears are linked. These forces where they occur are probably motivating people to act or react with the same strength which we find in incest, yet their range of occurrence is not as universal.

In general, marriage is most common between partners chosen from those more similar than different in social and other characteristics, even though societies no longer live in geographic or social isolation. The principle of endogamy or marrying within certain groups, either culturally distinctly specified or left vague, is found in all societies, traditional or modern.

As the significance of kinship and family fades in societies like ours and increasingly in many others, and as cultural rules in other respects weaken, marriages become more and more individualized. Under those conditions, marriages become experiments with nontraditional and unfamiliar behavior, not governed by rules which can be made explicit from one person to another. Where clear cultural rules no longer guide mate selection and many other aspects of the marriage relationship, what forces act on marriage behavior of people? A brief review of some academic arguments about principles of marriage choice may help to see intercultural marriage in perspective as one outcome of diminishing stringent cultural rules about appropriate mates.

The question: "In marriage does it happen 'like marries like' or that 'opposites attract' or is there some other principle?" has guided the research of Robert Winch, a sociologist. Given the basic and universal forces of incest regulation, the answer to this question may help to illustrate whether intercultural marriage is "natural" or a violation of some forces at the level of individual psychological functioning or at the level of social considerations. The investigation of the nature of complementarity in mate selection suggests that the sociological notion of homogamy, in which like tends to marry like, is in conflict with the notion of heterogamy, in which opposites attract. The latter, specifically tied to the psychoanalytic view, proposes that there is a tendency to seek in the marriage partner a person whose qualities are felt to compensate for those lacking in oneself. These qualities can be both positive or negative, a dominant person seeking a dependent partner, for example. The negative aspects of this selective principle relate to the psychological burden placed on one partner to help make up for psychological deficiencies in the other. Although sociological studies based on an investigation of American middle-class families do not lay claim to the development of universally applicable theories, it seems clear that complementarity in

6

marriage or the balancing of similarities and differences along several dimensions, is functional in marriages where other rules do no override such psychological considerations. But while complementarity seems to be important, such studies do not tell us what happens when the homogamy principle or the tendency to seek sufficient common grounds in religion, ethnic identification, and other social characteristics, is surrendered by an increasing number of marriages to a greater emphasis on the dissimilar or heterogamy principle.

In general, even where cultural rules specifying eligible partners weaken, other more informal rules continue to operate based on sociological and psychological factors, such as racial and generational considerations, similarity, and geographical proximity. A more specific theory of mate selection proposes three stages as crucial criteria for the functioning marriage in the absence of specific cultural rules: the stimulus stage, the values comparison stage and the role stage. Stimulus refers to the perception of the other's physical, social, mental, or reputational attributes. It is considered a stage because stimulus factors determine the first behavioral actions with regard to the potential marriage partner. This is followed by the values stage in which a couple "may compare their attitudes towards life, politics, sex, and the role of men and women in society and marriage." In the final role stage, actual role relationships for the couple are worked out, according to this theory. Although not stated in those terms, it is suggested that compatibility in all three areas has an equal force or function as more stringent cultural criteria in which, for example, stimulus value may be very narrowly defined. In any case, while this theory is not used in our book, there are some parallel assumptions in the chapters that follow. As in many marriage and mating discussions it seems as though here, too, common sense and clinical insights contribute as much as systematic research results to a useful understanding of the phenomena.

In the constant contacts of modern societies where communications take place at a variety of levels through writing, print, electronic means, and population movements, culture continues to be a significant context for human behavior but in a broader, more permissive, more flexible way. Intercultural marriage is one example of change. By definition, intercultural marriage is not a cultural form of marriage. It is a phenomenon of large scale migratory, either temporary or permanent movements of people. Where it occurs, it has been and still is considered to be a deviant form of marriage. But as with other cultural deviancies which have gradually become accepted because they are so common, this may some day be the case with intercultural marriage. In Hawaii, the rising number of marriages between individuals who grew up in families of quite divergent traditions and identifications has made intercultural marriage an accepted practice. This is not true everywhere.

Acceptance is only a step toward regularity. Intercultural marriage may create problems for spouses and offspring which ultimately come to the attention of the clinician. This is what we mean by the consequences or "implications" of intercultural marriage. Again, we find ourselves on shifting grounds. Problems are not the exclusive domain of intercultural or interracial marriages. Marriages between individuals of quite similar backgrounds run into difficulties. But the problems of intercultural marriage are somewhat unique, though they need not be more serious than marriage problems in more conventionally assorted couples.

The authors in this book imply that there are certain special hazards to intercultural marriage, and these are laid out in detail. The problems of intercultural marriages are real to the authors because they are frequently consulted by married couples of different cultural backgrounds. Professional insights are based on clinical experiences, while the explanations are based on the authors' general knowledge as behavioral scientists. Ari Kiev, a psychiatrist, has made points similar to our arguments about the impact of vanishing practical guidelines to behavior that traditional marriage rules and prohibitions in stable and traditional cultures provided. He writes, "The absence of constraint is associated with an increase in anxiety and uncertainty about making choices as well as an increase in the chance for erroneous or impractical choices."

Risks beyond those for marriages in general can be traced to several dimensions of cultural differences. Some of these are quite obvious, others are subtle and as yet little understood. For instance, there is little argument about the importance of similar or at least compatible values in marriage partners. But values themselves are often tied to the meanings or associations people hold about specific events or actions. For example, a person, on the basis of learned cultural beliefs, may find it undesirable to let an infant crawl freely on the floor. This value may directly oppose that of another person who thinks it is good for the infant to be permitted to crawl. The basis for the negative value may be a belief that crawling is an animal characteristic, inappropriate for humans; the meaning of the positive value may relate to associations with the learning of free expression and movement. Although the meanings have different roots, they may both be powerful sources in reinforcing and maintaining the respective values and therefore associated behaviors. This example, taken from quite broadly known ethnographic studies of Balinese and Americans seems fairly simple and obvious. There are many others that could be analyzed in the respective value orientations of individuals and the meanings to which they are tied. Unless unusually introspective and able to sort out such differences, marriage partners from diverse cultural

8

backgrounds face a burden that is more severe than for those coming from similar cultural backgrounds. The areas to which such examples could be related are numerous, some more sensitive than others, in particular food and sex to name two. If potential mates do, indeed, compare values prior to marriage, then it may be assumed that value differences have been sorted out in such a way that adaptations to potential conflicts are possible, although common sense tells us that this ideal may not be reached in many instances.

Even subtler than values as a source of potential risks in intercultural marriage is behavior tied to out-of-awareness systems or nonverbal communications. Cultural rules and culturally supported values may not be immediately accessible to the individual's consciousness unless elicited by questioning by others. But they can be established with relative ease, and the individual can be made aware of the rules that he follows or the values that she holds. Culture also modulates the expressions of emotions and in this manner holds a powerful control over the interaction of two individuals or larger groups. Although the question of the range of panhuman emotions which have compatible expressions and those which are tied to particular cultural controls is still a subject of basic research with relatively little application to everyday problems, it is now quite widely accepted that the out-of-awareness behaviors found in facial display, in gestures, in the use of speech, and in tone of voice are very significant elements of communication. We may safely suggest that at this point in time intercultural married couples cannot expect much outside support in raising these important behavioral areas to their awareness prior to marriage, nor once they are married. We may speculate that given strong and binding sentiments and a relatively adequate adjustment in other respects, values, roles, and the arrangement of relationships with relatives, friends, and most of all offspring, problems in the nonverbal areas of communications can be adequately controlled. Such issues arising in an intercultural marriage may become greatly aggravated as out-of-awareness behavior generates strong negative feelings which distance the intercultural couple more than may be the case in conflicts of more homogeneous marriages.

Traditional societies have specialists who can respond to problems of people whether these are individual, psychological problems or interpersonal problems. They differ in their domain of competence and concentration from modern specialists who address their knowledge and skills to problems arising from interactions of people of different cultural backgrounds. The transcultural or cross-cultural clinician is a new type of specialist for whom there are no traditional parallels. Intercultural marriage is certainly not a recent innovation, but its scale is beyond anything that must have taken place in the past. What is more, the role of the ex-

9

pert, the clinical specialist in personal and interpersonal problems, for example, is increasing as other cultural supports diminish in significance.

The risks involved in intercultural marriage and the chances of problems which are outlined in this book, while specific to such marriage, are part of a more general experience of people of different cultural backgrounds who live together. Immigrants, students from abroad, Peace Corps volunteers or other overseas workers living outside enclaves in foreign places are examples. A variety of training and counseling approaches have been developed over the past years and are reported in a book edited by Pederson in which the authors describe clinical remedies which they have found useful in their own experiences. These clinical techniques, whether considered conseling or therapy, must include an ability to identify and include cultural dimensions such as rules for behavior, values, meanings, and beliefs. They must also include an ability to communicate across different cultural backgrounds, in addition to more conventional clinical skills. A good part of therapeutic efforts, therefore, may deal as much with an interpretation of the cultural differences of a couple, as with their marriage problems. For much as these are linked, just dealing with the marriage as such is not enough. The same applies to children of such unions. Because identity and other important developmental aspects in the child are linked to the cultural and social position of parents, the problems of such children may be somewhat different and require appropriate responses.

It is by no means implied in this volume that intercultural marriage is bad, wrong, or too risky, though it is assumed that there are risks. At least one author is specific about positive aspects of intermarriage. Individual identity is generally seen as being established partly on the basis of social recognition by others, and for this and related reasons, humans may function best psychologically in groups sharing identical or compatible life styles. It is generally recognized that we are dealing with a subject matter which is relatively new and in need of further exploration. Not considered, for example, is the case of a person who intentionally marries outside the parental cultural group in order to seek, through intermarriage, an independent identity. A woman may consciously choose a marriage partner from a different group than the one in which she grew up in order to gain through this experience a springboard for a new and strongly independent identity as a woman. An unpublished paper about a woman of Japanese background married to a Caucasian suggests that in order to enable his wife to reach her goal, "this Caucasian (the husband), however, must be relatively free of close family ties himself so that restrictions are not imposed on the marriage, and he must tolerate his wife's continued search for identity which may include more than one 'false start'."

We have introduced intercultural marriage by attempting to put the topic into a general context of marriage, and of culture as a concept important for the understanding of human group and individual behavior. In so doing, we found that there are no precise referents for intercultural marriage, nor for any of the related phenomena such as culture. But a general description of the domain with which the chapters in this volume deal may help to delineate intercultural marriage and its implications as a special topic within the larger range of marriage, family, child, development, and the need for counseling and other types of clinical interventions. The specific point was made that traditional society provided rules and constraints in marriage as in other areas of human behavior. By implication, such a society also provided culturally mediated channels to deal with problems of marriage and related matters. In modern society with its broad contacts of people and opportunities for marrying outside the immediate group there is a need for the specialist and for special approaches. These are just beginning to emerge as the problems of intercultural marriage come into focus and basic knowledge about them is developed. In that sense, this book is a pioneering effort for those involved in clinical practice, or for those considering marriage across cultural boundaries, or for those who are already married.

REFERENCES

De Vos, G. Social stratification and ethnic pluralism: An overview from the perspective of psychological anthropology. *Race* 13:435-460, 1972

Hostetler, J. A. *Amish Society.* Baltimore, Maryland: Johns Hopkins Press, 1963.

Hostetler, J. A. and Huntington, G. E. *The Hutterites in North America.* New York: Holt, Rinehart, Winston, 1967.

Kiev, A. The psychiatric implications of interracial marriage. In *Interracial Marriage: Expectations and Realities.* Edited by I. R. Stuart and L. Edwin. New York: Grossman Publishers, 1973.

Mead, M. and MacGregor, F. C. *Growth and Culture.* New York: G. P. Putnam's Sons, 1951.

Murstein, B. I. A theory of marital choice applied to interracial marriage. In *Interracial Marriage: Expectations and Realities.* Edited by I. R. Stuart and L. Edwin. New York: Grossman Publishers, 1973.

Pederson, P., et al. *Counseling Across Cultures.* Honolulu: The University Press of Hawaii, 1976.

Stuart, I. R. and Edwin, L. *Interracial Marriage: Expectations and Realities.* New York: Grossman Publishers, 1973.

Winch, R. *Mate Selection.* New York: Harper Brothers, 1958.

Wolf, A. P. Childhood association, sexual attraction, and the incest taboo: A Chinese case. *American Anthropologist* 68:883-898, 1966.

2
Marriage: Universals

Linda Alexander, Ph.D.

Marriage expresses the rich diversity of all human institutions. Each culture or human group defines marriage uniquely and each individual within a marriage experiences it idiosyncratically. We see that marriage, across cultures, may be polygamous or monogamous, heterosexual or homosexual, political, economic, and romantic. It may be incestuous, it may be dictated by law, religion, or whim. It may be prohibited, preferred, or prescribed for a multitude of reasons. People in all times and everywhere have experimented with the potentialities offered by marriage and have produced a rich history of variation. It is difficult to reduce this history and this multifaceted institution to its universals.

But the reduction is a necessary precedent to the analysis of specific kinds of marriages. Knowing what is essential to this institution lets us know when a marriage is normal, and when it is not, when it is good, and when it is not. Knowing what is essential to marriage lets us make judgments.

What then are marriage universals? It has been suggested that marriage universally imposes sexual restraints on its participants. Yet there are marriages in which sexuality is not confined to the married persons, and there are also sexless marriages, which we might be hasty to judge as normal or not, good or not, or to disqualify as instances of marriage. Few features appear to characterize any and all marriages. Is the term "marriage" perhaps a semantic flop? Maybe there is an exception to everything we might propose as a defining characteristic of marriage, as essential to it.

But something lets us agree when people are married and when they aren't. Some definite quality or pattern identifies marital relationships as distinct from other kinds of relationships. We don't confuse a life-long relationship between close friends with marriage, although we may appreciate the similarities between the two kinds of relationships.

We will look at one chracteristic of marriage which may be nearly universal, the characteristic of duration. Marriages, for all their diversity in form and content, are intended to endure, even unto the death of the participants. This intended permanence of the relationship has various consequences. While this is a general and obvious near-universal, its consequences are interesting and less obvious.

Need Fulfillment

The first main correlate with a permanent or life-long bond between two or more people in marriage is that this arrangement must meet a broad range of needs. The durability of the relationship requires that important wishes and preferences be met: otherwise the arrangement would be trivial. What is interesting is the different ways people and societies divide the spectrum of human needs and assign some to marriage for their fulfillment.

For purposes of simpler statements, we can compare the total spectrum of human needs to beads on a rosary or interval marks on a yardstick. Each person might list his or her needs: the need for food, warmth, security, for trust and acceptance, for creativity and achievement, for companionship and sex. Each society and each individual marks off some of these need items and assigns them to marriage for their gratification. The remainder of the "beads" are counted in some other contexts; those needs not expected to be fulfilled in marriage are dealt with by means of other strategies. The other strategies each married individual uses may be prescribed or sanctioned by his or her culture and social system, in which case their use will be relatively guilt-free and appropriate. Or the extramarital alternatives a person selects may not be socially approved, causing guilt and malaise to be associated with their use.

We know of cultures which assign marriage the task of fulfilling almost all human needs. We know too of those societies where marriage is not expected to provide much human satisfaction and within any given social system we will find differences in expectations for married women and married men. These various cultural expectations regarding marriage may be reasonable and attainable, or inappropriate and unrealistic. There is regardless, always acknowledgment that *all* human needs can-

13

not be gratified in marriage. Extramarital alternatives will always be necessary and these are either openly sanctioned or implied by society.

For example, the adventure and romance of courtship experiences may be expected to characterize a marriage on one level, while on another level, the following sort of comment denies this.

> When two people are under the influence of the most violent, most insane, most delusive and most transient of passions, they are required to swear that they will remain in that excited, abnormal, and exhausting condition continuously until death do them part. (George Bernard Shaw, Preface *Getting Married.*)

Societies vary in the extent to which they permit "sham" to pervade their institutions. An institution such as marriage may well be intended to meet needs it cannot and does not meet. The alternatives people will employ to fulfill themselves may be as institutional as marriage.

Tautologically, the common and periodic human need to not be married can never be fulfilled in matrimony.

> And yet, no matter how the night
> May chain me with its ring of longing,
> The pull of separation is still stronger
> And I have a beckoning passion for the clean break.
> (Boris Pasternak, "Explanation", *Dr. Zhivago*)

It is ironic that marriage may generate a powerful desire to not be married.

Our point is that marriage is limited in the needs it can fulfill and that there must always be alternatives to this relationship. These are extramarital and sanctioned or not sanctioned, implicitly or explicitly. Most societies will have rules regarding which alternatives are not acceptable. And because marriage is intended to be a permanent bond and not a transient relationship, marriage itself will generate needs. The needs not met in marriage and the needs generated by marriage require extramarital alternatives for their fulfillment.

Marital Redundancy

The permanence of the marital bond usually results in ongoing, repetitious, frequent interactions between the marriage participants. Monogamy and polygamy differ in the frequency and number of repetitive interactions. For simplicity, we will hereafter refer primarily to monogamous male-female relationships, since there are more common. But our discussions are meant to apply, with appropriate qualification, to all forms of marriage. And in all types of marriages, interaction between the spouses is of a sort regardless of the type or marriage.

The perseverance of interaction produces redundant and stereotypic exchanges between husband and wife. Over time, differences in attitude, expectation, and communication diminish. While any person's maturation and learning would tend to make him or her disparate and unique, they become the mutual experiences of two people when they occur in an intimate, repetitious and ongoing marriage. In their routine and increasingly ritual interactions, married people grow to be very similar in many areas.

> He knew exactly how things would go: it had happened so often before. He rehearsed every word, going back into his office, locking his desk, going down to his car . . . I shall go in and I'll say, "Good evening, Sweetheart," and she'll say, "Good evening, darling. What kind of day?" and I'll talk and talk . . . (Graham Greene, *The End of the Affair*)

The habituated relationship becomes, by definition, highly redundant and therefore uninformative. The word "information" is used here in its particular sense of being analogous to the measure of improbability of occurrence of a message. The more frequent or redundant the occurrence of a message or event, the less informative it becomes. This is a major tenet of information theory.

Some needs are met by relational redundancy. The needs to predict, to experience certainty, to economize choices and to minimize anxiety are well met in such a circumstance. The rich unspoken acceptance and trust that may develop in marriage are only possible because of its permanency and redundancy. The efficacy of marriage in meeting these needs is probably unsurpassed by any other human convention.

But another consequence of marital redundancy is that it requires a great deal of energy to maintain a steady state. The more redundant or ritualized any part of a relationship, the more potent and meaningful any divergence from its regular pattern becomes. The repetition permits the possibility of highly informative alternatives with only minimal change. Redundancy in marriage is need gratifying and desired. Its preservation requires that the relationship be monitored to some extent to prevent novelty. In other words, the system develops a high potential for instability and energy expenditure is required to prevent variation and to maintain a steady state in many areas.

Novelty, of course, can also be need gratifying in marriage, but when endorsed as a pattern or ritual, it only moves the redundancy to a higher level. Spouses will then agree, implicitly or explicitly, on how much divergence from pattern or novelty will be acceptable or discounted.

> There is only one man in my life who has ever . . . made me happy . . . George . . . who keeps learning the games we play as quickly as I can change the rules. (Edward Albee, *Who's Afraid of Virginia Woolf*)

Another consequence of the repetition of marital interaction is satisfaction of those needs for predictability, certainty, security, acceptance, trust, and the like. Each day of marriage further establishes the patterns of relationship which gratify those needs. Yet each day of that investment depletes the marriage to some degree of novelty, newness, adventure, and curiosity.

As security needs are periodically or increasingly satiated, needs for new stimuli are periodically or increasingly unmet.

> There were kitchens and stoves with fires in them . . . And in the midst of them all were scattered hundred-yen pieces, domestic animals, children, sex, promissory notes, adultery, incense burners, souvenir photos, and . . . It goes on, terrifyingly repetitive. One could not do without repetition in life, like the beating of the heart, but it was also true that the beating of the heart was not all there was to life. (Kobo Abe, *The Women in the Dunes*)

The less analytical description of this state is "boredom."

To recapitulate, some needs are not met in marriage, and some are generated by marriage. A primary need generated by the redundancy and repetition—the boredom—of marriage, is the need for difference. We should qualify here that human needs are not static items like beads on a rosary, nor finite like marks on a measuring stick. What we are summarily calling "needs" are exceedingly complex responsive states of organisms in dynamic arrangements and interactions. These changing states are reflected in changing preferences and behaviors. But marriage is intended to be permanent. This overriding prescription is not always fulfilled: separation or divorce may terminate the marital arrangement. When the marriage continues, however, extramarital alternatives must be utilized, to satisfy needs not met in marriage and needs produced by marriage.

Extramarital Alternatives

We should now consider what extramarital alternatives are available to spouses as corrective, supplemental or compensatory resources for need gratification.

Complex games, strategies, and delaying techniques are used to perpetuate marriage in every society, and the natural limitations of the marital relationship requires recourse to nonmarital strategies; their use is not itself an indication of good, bad, healthy, pathological, or other diagnoses of the state of a particular marriage, but a deficit of all marriages to some degree. What we will observe, however, are fallacies in the use of any one strategy, and the potential for destroying the marriage that each extramarital alternative contains.

We should note that a person cannot be married and at the same time single. For the single or unmarried person, a wide range of need-fulfillment alternatives exist. For the married person, we propose that only four kinds of supplemental or corrective alternatives exist.

All extramarital activities which repeat the structure and characteristics of the marriage are "symmetrical" strategies. Symmetrical describes a relationship between two things where the same kinds of behavior or attributes are expressed or exchanged. The things in this case are the marital domain and extramarital domain. When one gives them the same structure or attributes, one places them in symmetrical relation to one another.

There are two basic kinds of symmetry between marriage and its alternatives. The first is colloquially called "the affair", biblically named "adultery." This alternative may be socially sanctioned or prohibited.

Adulterous alternatives usually repeat much of the marriage structure and for this reason stand in competitive relation to the marriage itself. Male/female roles, economic patterns, sexual relations, sentiment, intimacy, and usually a serious attachment are repeated in the affair. Because these characteristics often describe marriage, the adulterous strategy is usually subtractive from the marriage it intends to supplement.

> He had stayed so long that one might wonder whether he had forgotten his wife and children. He stayed not because he could not leave Komako nor because he did not want to. He had simply fallen into the habit of waiting for those frequent visits. (Yasunari Kawabata, *Snow Country*)

On the other hand, the affair can initially correct marital boredom simply because redundant interactional patterns have not been established in the affair. Novelty, excitement, risk taking, adventure, and new stimulation are all components, apart from whether or not the affair is conducted clandestinely or is forbidden. As the affair proceeds over time, it too much acquires the habituation and mutualization of a long-term interaction, and while it may continue to meet other needs, the need for change and novelty will again be unsatisfied.

> They knew each other too well to feel that breathless wonder which makes to joy of possession a hundred times more intense. She was as satiated with him as he was tired of her. She was beginning to find in adultery all the dullness of marriage. (Gustave Flaubert, *Madame Bovary*)

Once this particular symmetrical paradigm is adopted, new affairs can always be initiated to attempt to reduce redundancy. However, the fallacy in this is that it generates a new repetitive pattern.

> The speed with which she moved from one milieu to another, from one man, place, date to another, was staggering . . . and every action ended in error, guilt, repentence. How often I remember—"Darling, this time it will be different, I promise you." (Lawrence Durrell, *Justice*)

The other symmetrical strategy is the mutual participation of the spouses in revitalization of their relationship by minimizing areas of redundancy and maximizing change and novelty. We will persist in calling this an "extramarital" resolution because it extends far beyond the scope of marriage: it attempts to meet all human needs in one relationship. Bizarre or extreme sexual practices are sometimes an outcome; psychotherapy, parapsychology, new joint enterprises of many sorts are employed to negate the routine and regular responses more typical of marriage. Extramarital resources are incorporated into the union and the participants mutually engage in domain of activity not usually subsumed by any definition of marriage.

> If they try to act like citizens
> And rent them a nice little flat
> About the third night
> They're invited to fight
> By a sub-gun's rat-tat-tat.
>
> Some day they'll go down together;
> They'll bury them side by side;
> To few it'll be grief—
> To the law a relief—
> But it's death for Bonnie and Clyde.
> (David Newman and Robert Benton, *Bonnie and Clyde*)

This tactic can put redundancy and security at risk, essentially channeling the energy devoted to maintenance of routine into the more difficult arena of maintaining a frequently changing state. But again, persistence in this strategy or any other is a higher-order redundancy; while increasing the domain of joint activity it also increases the potential for first-level boredom.

Societies vary in their sanction of symmetrical resolutions. In some societies the affair is sanctioned for men and not women, sometimes being limited to the use of prostitutes. In others, neither spouses may appropriately use this form of correction. Those social systems which assign the marital relationship little accountability for human need fulfill-

18

ment would not likely permit revitalization tactics, while those cultures putting great responsibility on marriage would reward that alternative but possibly not the affair.

An alternative to repeating the marriage structure in extramarital contexts is to supplement the marriage with entirely different sorts of relationships. This is the complementary approach. "Complementary" describes a relationship between two things which exchange or express different behaviors or attributes. Again, the things of reference here are the marital and extramarital spheres of action. There are two paradigms.

One is to generate an active set of social or professional relationships with members of other groups, or with persons for whom no marital inclinations or sentiments hold. The elaboration of extramarital relationships of this order can meet many needs not satisfied in marriage and is not as potentially repetitious as the symmetrical affair: the existing marriage relationship structure is not duplicated. On the other hand, every persistent activity develops its own redundant patterns; acquaintances and professions can become boring in their own right. Or, the extramarital activity can become more absorbing and engaging than the marriage, ceasing to be supplemental and threatening to replace it.

Every minute he was awake he was practicing Medicine. The demands of the day were inflexible, exterior and this situation freed him from any nudge of guilt for doing what he most desired to the exclusion of every other human activity and the expense of any other human who might emotionally be involved in his life actions. (Morton Thompson, *Not as a Stranger*)

The second complementary method is to elaborate separately and alone one's own unique, creative, and nonmarital interests. Painting, writing, music, carpentry, sailing, fantasy and a diversity of hobbies and creative activities may serve to meet many intrapersonal needs. When these idiosyncratic activities are periodically punctuated with social approbation and acknowledgment, they may provide a source for extramarital satisfaction, or again, a replacement for marital activity.

If my wife says one word too many, how could I possibly be in the mood to play the SANTURI? . . . To play the SANTURI you have to give everything up to it, d'you understand? (Nikos Kanzantzakis, *Zorba the Greek*)

Again, societies vary in their preference for the complementary resolution of marriage problems. In many, the social complement is provided in institutional form, and in others, more especially for men, in the form of professional or work roles. Each culture provides a prescription, whether implicitly or explicitly, which utilizes some combination of the above four extramarital alternatives. But with or without cultural sanction, each individual in a marriage has the ultimate choice and the concommitant guilt or pleasure to weigh in the choosing. Between any husband and wife sixteen possibilities for agreement or disagreement exist with respect to these alternatives. The mathematical possibilities suggest that most marriages can resolve the boredom problem at least by shifting to new combinations of the four alternatives, given cultural prescription, social propriety, and individual choice.

One choice on this scale is to select none of the extramarital alternatives. Nonresolution of marital boredom and nonfulfillment of unmet needs has clearly been sanctioned in some times and places. For example, much American literature epitomizes the frustration, resignation, impotence and lack of vitality of husbands and wives who do not meet their needs within or without their marital union. Ingrown sadomasochistic relationships gain classic status in works such as *Who's Afraid of Virginia Woolf.* One might conjecture that remaining within a paradox has such a consequence, and that choosing none of the alternatives is degenerative. Designing the marriage as a "nonmarriage," with dominant patterns of separate professions, separate vacations, separate acquaintances, and separate interests, in another choice. The latter tends to deny that a marriage actually exists and has its own resultant problems.

Multiple choices and alternatives do exist to provide compensation for the deficits of matrimony; selection among them is governed by an equally large complex of variations, some of which are explored in other chapters of this book the nul case is, of course, always available: to not be married at all.

A Roman divorced from his wife, being highly blamed by his friends, who demanded, "was she not chaste? Was she not fair? Was she not fruitful?" holding out his shoe, asked them whether it was not new and well made. "Yet," added he, "none of you can tell where it pinches me." (Plutarch, *Aemilius Paulus*)

REFERENCES

Abe, Kobo. *The Woman in the Dunes.* Translated from the Japanese by E. Dale Saunders. New York: Knopf, 1964.

Albee, Edward. *Who's Afraid of Virginia Woolf?* New York: Atheneum, 1962.

Durrell, Lawrence. *Justine.* New York: Pocket Books, 1961.

Flaubert, Gustave. *Madame Bovary.* Translated from the French by Francis Steegmuller. New York: Modern Library, 1958.

Greene, Graham. *The End of the Affair.* New York: The Viking Press, 1951.

Kawabata, Yasunari. *Snow Country.* Translated from the Japanese by Edward G. Seidensticker. New York: Knopf, 1969.

Kazantzakis, Nikos. *Zorba, the Greek.* Translated by Carl Wildman. New York: Simon and Schuster, 1959.

Newman, David and Benton, Robert. *Bonnie and Clyde,* screenplay published in *The Bonnie and Clyde Book.* Compiled and edited by Sandra Wake and Nicola Hayden. New York: Simon and Schuster, 1972.

Pasternak, Boris. *Dr. Zhivago.* Translated from the Russian by Max Hayward and Manya Harari. New York: Modern Library, 1958.

Plutarch. Aemilius Paulus. *In Plutarch's Lives.* Vol. 6. Cambridge: Harvard University Press, 1943.

Shaw, George Bernard. *Getting Married. In Complete Plays, with prefaces.* New York: Dodd, Mead, 1962.

Thompson, Morton. *Not as a Stranger.* New York: Signet Books, 1954.

3

Intercultural Perspectives on Mate Selection

Danilo E. Ponce, M.D.

In earlier times, the rules governing mate selection were relatively simple, fixed, and allowed little room for changes or deviations. In essence, the basic rule was that one marries one's own kind. The definition of "kind" varied from group to group depending on the common bond(s) that held the group together; be it religion, culture, family, country, color of skin, professional identities, socioeconomic status or geographic propinquity. Given this basic rule, individual say-so in the matter was limited merely to who among one's own kind one chose as a mate. In some instances, even this one choice was not allowed, as in cultures or socioeconomic classes where betrothal arrangements were made at birth. Transactions were quite straightforward, even though prescribed rites and rituals may have been elaborated and quite often conducted by the parents or their representatives.

The advent of the modern era ushered profound changes into this relatively closed system of mate selection. Two very distinct developments helped introduce these changes: (1) spectacular technological advances in the field of communication and transportation dramatically increased the exposure, commingling and cross-fertilization of hitherto insular groups, races or cultures; and (2) following an exponential increase in contact amongst peoples, there understandably followed drastic revisions and changes in traditions, customs, beliefs, practices, and institutions. What had been taboos and impossibilities in previous times became contemporary possibilities and actualities. Both of these developments are part of very rapid and dramatic changes in modern life that have collectively come to be known as "future shock" phenomenon.

The impact of future shock in terms of mate selection can be seen in the tremendous increase of the rate at which individuals marry others that are not of their own kind. It is now commonplace for nobility to marry commoners, for a Chinese to marry a Japanese; for a black to marry a white; for a Jew to marry a Catholic; for a boss to marry the secretary. The combinations are endless. Future shock has had its effect not only in opening up marital opportunities, but also in stimulating a questioning of the very notion of marriage itself. As an institution, it is undergoing very close scrutiny from some quarters. For example, when one spoke about "mate selection" before, it was taken for granted that one was referring to heterosexual bonding. Currently, homosexual pairs are demanding the right to be married. It is conceivable that in the near future one will have to become more explicit when one talks about mates. One can enumerate other examples of drastic changes in the way marriage and practices surrounding marriage are now undergoing modifications. For instance, some Catholic priests are suggesting revision of the rule regarding celibacy; doctors are marrying their patients; anthropologists are marrying members of the tribe they are studying, and so on. Many modern couples have dispensed with the institution altogether and have decided to live together rather than be bound by the perceived constraints of a formal marriage. Indeed, there have been remarkable changes from earlier beliefs and practices regarding both the selection of a mate and of marriage itself.

However, these conceptual shifts are still far from becoming norms. The average, expectable person in our time will still think of getting married some day, and is still probably thinking of getting married to his/her own kind. Thus much of the discussions which follows will deal with perspectives on mate selection, with particular emphasis on the intercultural dimension.

Basic Considerations

It would seem from the bulk of literature written thus far about mixed marriages that there is something not quite right about the event or the participants in the event. One gets this feeling from both sides of the camp—the camp that presents impressive statistics designed to show why the coupling is doomed to failure right from the start and the other that almost embarrassingly tries to show that mixed marriages may be one of the healthiest things that can ever happen to anybody, or at least present no more of a problem than homogeneous ones. As usual, the

23

truth is probably somewhere in the golden mean. The point is not so much where the truth lies, as an examination of the attitudes that are brought to bear on a given phenomenon. If one comes from the vantage point that says this is either abnormal and deviant, or healthy and optimal, then the dice is already loaded. Only recently are we beginning to realize the import of this observation. In sociology, for instance, there is emerging a point of view known as labeling theory; in educational psychology, the so-called Rosenthal or pygmalion effect; and in psychiatry and allied sciences, the general system theory. Essentially, the theme common to all these conceptual approaches is that the observer cannot help but influence the nature of the observed; and that if we are not careful in scrutinizing our preconceived beliefs, notions, and biases, then the process we will be indulging in is not so much a study but rather a simple validation of what we are looking for—a self-fulfilling prophecy. Caveat number one, then, as it applies to a discussion about the process of mate selection from a different culture, is to insure that we do not get unwittingly caught in assuming that there is something "wrong" in choosing a mate from another culture.

Caveat number two is that no one conceptual approach can fully and satisfactorily explain and account for all the factors involved in choosing a mate from a different culture. Most of the papers written around and about the subject thus far explore only one or two dimensions: the intrapsychic, psychoanalytic, organismic or motivational dimension and the extrapsychic, sociocultural, group, or environmental dimension. Like the nature versus nurture controversies that have permeated other areas of studies in the behavioral sciences, we cannot seem to get away from an either/or approach. A reasonably good approach must view things not only as multidetermined but, more importantly, show how these factors relate and interact with each other—the so-called area of the between. Showing how these factors are not necessarily mutually exclusive but complementary may fill in some of the conceptual gaps that occur if each of these approaches are taken separately. Using this approach we can now begin to explain why even the most fertile intrapsychic field, like neurotic complementarity, or the most propitious external circumstances, like propinquity, do not lead to marriage. There may be other overriding factors involved which we might miss if we persist in maintaining a myopic point of view.

Caveat number three is really a corollary of both caveats: the necessity of seeing that the process of deciding and choosing a mate from a different culture does not happen in a vacuum. Choosing a mate from a different culture is a process that is in flux, is subject to content, set, and setting.

Caveat number four is that the formal rites of marriage must be viewed merely as the culmination of the process that has been evolving since the couple first became aware of each other's existence and decided to pursue the relationship further. The evolutionary process of the relationship has clear-cut stages or phases: beginning, middle, and end (or another beginning as the case may be). Forces that were not so prominent or influential when the couple decided to pursue the relationship after the first encounter may now come to fore. Not all couples who become attracted to each other, even to the point of considering marriage, do eventually marry each other.

Bearing the aforementioned caveats in mind, a reasonably good conceptual model to use in trying to understand why person A from culture X chooses, decides, and actually marries person B from culture Y must, by necessity, address itself to different levels of conceptualization. Further, the model must show how each of the levels in turn relate to the others. This is not too dissimilar from Koestler's idea of the Janus effect in describing how one might talk of the relationship betwen parts and wholes in behavioral processes (Janus being the two-faced Roman god, one face looking inward, the other outwar.

The first level is the organismic, interpersonal, intrapsychic level. Here the level is reduced to all the significant forces that impel or drive a person from one culture to marry a person from a different culture. The flow of events here is from inside, out. This permits one to conceptualize, as Freud did, that marital choice stems essentially from the drive to marry someone similar to a previous love object such as one's father or mother, or one that offers nurturance and protection (anaclitic). The theorizing is mainly psychoanalytic or motivational in nature and answers the question, "Why?"

The second level is the environmental, interpersonal, extrapsychic level. Here one takes into account all the forces that impinge on the individual that are outside his/her skin. Thus, one speaks not only about the physical environment that is readily observable and demonstrable such as external characteristics of the person from a different culture, but also the not so readily observable and demonstrable psychosocial field such as culture, religion, and class.

Attraction based on physical characteristics which leads one to marry somebody from a different culture is probably best understood on the basis of personal preference and idiosyncracy. As much as some persons prefer tall, heavy-set, well-endowed, blue-eyed blondes, there will be others who prefer short, frail, flat-chested, brown-eyed brunettes. The role that culture might play in this is the cultural stereotyping (for example, American women are seen as pushy and aggressive, German women are really feminine, etc.) that can whet one's expectations on the one hand or make for instant repugnance on the other. This is particularly striking as it applies to the sexual and dominance-submission areas. In part, physical characteristics of persons from a given race or culture could easily reinforce these preconceived notions and fantasies. A tall, Nordic, blue-eyed blonde from Sweden lends herself very well to visions of free and unlimited sensuality while a petite, demure, and retiring Oriental girl lends herself more to fantasies of gentility and submissive passivity.

A distinction must be made at this point between physical attraction that leads to a casual liaison or even a "semicommitted" relationship that does not lead to marriage, and one that culminates in marriage. Just because one is attracted physically to another does not mean one is thinking of the other as a potential mate. Here again, culture seems to heavily influence one's eventual choice and decision. An Oriental man, for example, might consider a Western woman for sexual partnership but will think long and hard once marriage is presented for consideration. It is at this point that he begins to think not only of himself but of the impact his marrying somebody from a different culture will have on his friends and his immediate relatives.

The influence of the psychosocial field, such as culture, religion, and class, is best appreciated in terms of the negative set of rules and taboos, the violation of which implies dire social consequences. Thus, one does not marry somebody from an alien culture, a different religion, or a different socioeconomic class. The consequences are generally social in nature, but can wreak considerable individual havoc and misery as in well-documented effects of taboo violation. One risks social isolation, economic deprivation, and becoming an outcast from one's religion. Classic literature has exploited this theme over and over again. The characters that enact the drama are different, but the thread remains the same—rich boy-poor girl, Jew-gentile, Westerner-Oriental, god-mortal. The denouement of these relationships more or less reveals the disfavor with which such mixing is viewed; one or both participants generally suffer a tragic fate.

The third level is the time-space level. Last but certainly not least is the dimension provided by time and space. In this context, we are talking about ontogenetic and epigenetic time, an individual person's age and stage of development; phylogenetic time, roughly, the sociocultural ethos and Weltanschauung that are current and prevailing, indicative of a given culture's stage of development in the social-evolutionary scale; and dyadic time, the length of time the couple have known each other and consequently, where they are as far as the status of their relationship is concerned.

It is certainly a truism that decisions and choices made by an individual vary depending on his cognitive and emotional stage of development. The kinds of choices made by an adolescent are certainly quite different from those of a middle-aged or senior citizen. An adolescent may marry somebody from another culture as part of a rebellion against established authority figures in his/her life. A jaded, middle-aged person may do so as part of his/her continuing search for excitement or escape from boredom and ennui; a senior citizen may do so simply out of loneliness or expediency.

The prevailing sociocultural ethos has a great deal to do with the ease and facility or the difficulty of accepting an intercultural marriage. In these so-called liberated times, previously strong family and group affiliations loosen up or dissolve, taboos and unspoken rules and regulations lose their potency, and there are less constraints or pressures exerted on the individual. This is reinforced by the fact that the increase of geographic mobility decreases the necessity of dealing with one's immediate roots and family ties on a day-to-day basis. However, there are some cultures that are seemingly unaffected by the liberalized spirit of the times. Wherever they are, they still look upon the mother culture as a source when it is time to choose a mate. There are some immigrants who still insist to "going back home" in order to marry.

As previously mentioned, the chronological tracing of the couple's relationship is important since forces operating in cases of "love at first sight" may be quite different from forces that eventually determine whether the initial attraction is of sufficient strength and durability to insure marriage. Very briefly, some of the forces that may be operating in the beginning phase of a relationship are: (1) Preestablished values, biases, stereotypes, and idiosyncracies; if one has been conditioned to abhor anything alien or foreign, then there is low probability for the relationship to proceed any further. On the other hand, if one habitually relishes anything new and novel, then the chances for the relationship to continue become much higher. (2) Set and setting; the mental set and the setting play a heavy role in inhibiting or facilitating the alliance. This probably explains the casualness in which summer, shipboard, holiday, and war romances are established. (3) Personality of the individuals; here neurotic conflicts, current mental status, status of one's self-esteem, prestige, and pride system, ego-ideals, and so on, are operating. An individual may decide to have an affair with a person from another culture, using that person as a symbol for the acting out of parent-child conflicts;

as a potential solution to getting out of a distressing condition like poverty; as a way to escape depression, loneliness, boredom, alienation, or social isolation; as a cushion to an already sagging self-esteem. (4) Physical-sexual attractiveness. one's own biological and sexual preferences. (5) Age-stage of personality development.

Once the getting-to-know-you phase is over, assuming that the couple agrees to continue the relationship, the couple slides into the middle phase where the issues become clearly interpersonal. This is the period of time when behavioral, cognitive, emotional, social, and cultural conflicts become prominent and demand resolutions. Generally, this phase makes or breaks the relationship. Representative issues are: (1) Communication patterns; who talks to whom, when, where, how, and in what way. (2) Attitudes; personal, familial, and cultural stances become more clearly focused, particularly on such items as sex, man-woman roles, money, and religion. Usually this is a double-edged sword in that attitudinal stereotyping is utilized as a rationalization to either foster a nonexistent interpersonal conflict or to dampen the impact of an existing one. It is not uncommon for couples to say, well, what do you expect from a Chinese person? (Irish, French, etc.), when the problem may inherently be the individual. (3) Minor flaws ignored or not noticed during the initial phase of the relationship suddenly assume an importance that was not there before, for instance personal hygiene, dress, and eating and sleeping habits. (4) Pragmatic issues, less romantic, day-to-day issues like who pays for dining out, who entertains whose friends, which movie or T.V. program to watch, who and what has priority. (5) Motivating factors based on needs; Maslow's concept of hierarchy of needs is extremely helpful at this phase of the relationship. To a certain extent, the continuation or the termination of the relationship at this point is contingent on each person satisfying or not satisfying needs as spelled out by Maslow: physical/physiological needs, safety/security needs, social needs, ego needs, and self-actualizing needs.

If the couple survives the interpersonal issues in the midddle phase and the gratifications of the relationship outweigh the frustations, marriage may now be considered as a possibility unless the couple's values and goals in life preclude marriage. Once marriage becomes a possibility, interpersonal factors fade into the background and the impact of the "significant others" becomes quite palpable. The third and final phase is ushered in with questions like: (1) What will my family, relatives, friends think/feel? (socio/economic-cultural factors); (2) How will he/she function as a father/mother, husband/wife, daughter-in-law/son-in-law? (societal roles); (3) Will I be accepted into his/her family? Will he/she be accepted into mine? Will our cultural differences be a problem? (4) If we have children, how shall we raise them? How shall we name them? (5) Which marriage rites shall we have?

The three phases in the couple's relationship are really a continuum and not as arbitrary as is being presented here. Depending on the couple, the phases may take a few weeks to a few years. The final decision to actually get married will depend on how the vectors of forces, pro or con, are weighed, balanced, and are acted on. For instance, a person may eventually decide to get married because fulfilling sexual needs is more important to him/her than any of the anticipated dire consequences involved in marrying somebody from a different culture.

Proximity plays a no less important role in selecting a mate from another culture. It has been observed in previous studies that nearness to and availability of a person (as in the case of war brides) enhances the chances of marital coupling. Propinquity in educational pursuits and work/leisure situations is another factor that may advance the possibility of marriages.

Aside from circumstantial proximity, availability of eligible partners must also be considered. Whenever potential partners of the same group membership are rather scarce, as in the case of immigrants there is no choice but to consider other alternatives. Understandably then, exogamy is prone to occur in small cultural pockets surrounded by a bigger cultural mainstream.

A Gestalt: Seeing It as a Whole

To get a fairly comprehensive and accurate picture of what makes person A from culture X marry person B from culture Y, one must then adopt, by necessity, an ecosystem, organism-environment approach. The actual choice and the decision-making process that culminate in a person from one culture selecting a mate from another must be seen as a dynamic interplay of forces whereby the organism in its totality interacts with the environment. The organism and the environment in turn are contextually framed by time and space.

For instance, in order to get a good acccounting of what makes a particular Japanese man marry a particular French woman, one must raise questions like: What is going on inside his head (motives)? What does he expect to gain by marrying her (incentives)? Are there implicit or explicit group sanctioned rules and regulations that he is transcending and/or violating (cultural factors)? If so, and he is aware of these, what stronger factor(s) is operating that either pulls or pushes him to go ahead and pursue the relationship in spite of inferred adverse consequences meted out by his group? Is it because his group ties are not as potent anymore because of physical or psychological distance (immigration)? Where is he in terms of personality development (young, immature, mature)? Does a liasion with a woman from another culture represent a way of rebelling against his parents (intrapsychic, neurotic conflicts)? Does he have fantasies about French women (cultural stereotyping)? Do they work in the same office (propinquity, availability)? Have they just met or do they already have an affair going (stage of relationship)? These and similar questions along the same vein ought to be looked into in order to get a fairly comprehensive and valid answer. Parenthetically, the same line of questioning could apply as much to the French woman as to the Japanese man.

Seeing how the parts fit into the whole enables one to account for the facts that in some instances, even if the conditions are right in one area or level, stronger forces in other levels may cancel this level out. A Hawaiian beachboy strolling on the beach at Waikiki may be the perfect embodiment of a woman tourist's fantasy about a casual holiday affair, but other forces must be brought into focus if the question of mate selection is brought up as a possibility. Eventually, one of the levels, pro or con, becomes the stronger and will ultimately determine what course of action the couple will pursue. This is where social psychology theories like the balance theory of Fritz Heider, the cognitive dissonance theory of Leon Festinger, the exchange theory of Tannenbaum, and the conflict-resolution theories are extremely helpful in predicting eventual outcome for the couple.

It is not by accident that nowhere was the word love mentioned as a motivator for mate selection. Though some die-hard romanticists will want to proclaim that love is the great incentive for the development of bonds between people, it is rather hard to find two people who will agree on what they mean by the term. As an aside, contemporary attempts to put the phenomenon into a more scientific perspective has met with unexpected opposition from some respected quarters. In part, this is due to an almost ingrained resistance to talk about love in less than mystical or romantic terms. It is as if in trying to analyze and dissect, people feel that the essence is lost somewhere in the analysis. People will argue, what benefit will one derive in knowing that a rose is made up of such and such chemical compounds: There is a point there somewhere, particularly in these sensitive times when anything that vaguely hints of rationality or the scientific is viewed with suspicion. If love is believed by a significant number of people to be a potent force in the development of emotional and social bonds, then behavioral scientists have to somehow account for this phenomenon.

Using the model presented earlier, love would probably fit easily in any of the conceptual levels mentioned. In other words, love could mean: "you remind me of my mother"; "I'm alone and lonely and you are conveniently near and available"; "you are the perfect complement to satisfy my neurotic needs to rebel and be punished"; "I am sexually attracted to you"; "you are a solution to my economic problems"; "exotic is erotic is love"; and so forth and so on. In this context, "love" need not remain mystical and vague, it can indeed be operationalized, as some logical positivists would say.

Final Analysis: So What?

In our headlong rush toward making the world into one big global village where everybody is equal but different, we tend not to question what is going on as long as, in our minds, what is going on looks like one more step in meeting our utopian goal. This is particularly true in the area of exogamous marriages, and in our case, intercultural marriages. There is a noticeable discomfort when intercultural couples are asked what factors were influential in their decision to select each other as a mate, and perhaps rightfully so. Questions in and by themselves carry other messages. By posing the question, it is not difficult to understand that it could be easily interpreted as: "something is wrong with you"; or "you are going to have problems"; or "you are very bold and courageous in transgressing your cultural taboos." Further, the cultural context becomes an easy way to explain away difficulties and/or gratifications both couples may be experiencing in their marriages. It sets up a "no-win" proposition. If the marriage fails, it is generally attributed to cultural differences. If it succeeds, it is attributed to the couple's courage in acting on the basis of what they want in spite of cultural taboos. In any case, culture may at times assume unwarranted and undeserved importance.

It is easy enough to argue on the basis of studies made that mixed marriages are laboring under a handicap right from the start and couples from differing cultural backgrounds ought to be aware of this. On the other hand, as in any controversial issue, other studies can be as easily mastered to show exactly the opposite conclusions. In the final analysis, the value of delving into factors that enter into mate selection, particularly in couples of differing cultural backgrounds, is probably best appreciated by professionals who are in the business of helping people in the human services field. For these professionals, cultural variables must be considered as an important factor among other factors in the understanding of the relative success or failure of the marriage. Too, marriage in itself is already such a complicated process that a global understanding of the various forces involved would not only be desirable but almost mandatory.

REFERENCES

Adams, A. *Inter-racial Marriage in Hawaii.* New York: McMillan and Co., 1961.

Becker, H. *Outsiders: Studies in Sociology of Deviance.* New York: Free Press, 1963.

Brown, R. *Social Psychology.* Toronto: Collier, McMillan, 1967.

Cahnman, W. J. ed. *Intermarriage and Jewish Life: A Symposium.* New York: The Hertzl Press, 1963.

Druss, R. Foreign marriages in the military. *Psychiatric Quarterly* 39(2): 220-226, 1965.

Freud, S. Introduction to narcissium. *Collected Papers,* Vol. 4. London: Hogarth Press, 1943.

Gordon, A. *Intermarriage: Interethnic, Interfaith, Interracial.* Boston: Beacon Press, 1964.

Harris, T. G. Mr. chairman's hatchet job. *Psychology Today,* Vol. 8, No. 12, May, 1975.

Katz, A., et. al Residential propinquity and marital selection: A review of theory, method and fact. *Marriage and Family Living* 20:27-35, 1959.

Klemer, R. H. Marriage and family relationships. In *Social Factors in Mate Selection.* New York: Harper and Row, 1970.

Koestler, A. *The Ghost in the Machine.* New York: McMillan and Co., 1968.

Maslow, A. *Motivation and Personality.* New York: Harper, 1954.

Murstein, B., ed. *Theories of Attraction and Love.* New York: Springer Publishing Co., 1971.

Rosenberg, L. *Canada's Jews.* Montreal: Canadian Jewish Congress, 1939.

Rossenthal, R. et. al *Pygmalion in the Classroom.* New York: Holt, 1968.

Toffler, A. *Future Shock.* New York: Random House, 1970.

von Bertalannfy, L. *General System Theory.* New York: Geo. Brazillier, 1968.

Winch, R. et. al. The theory of complementary need in mate selection: An analytic and descriptive study. *American Sociological Review* 19:241-249, 1954.

4

Motivations for Intercultural Marriages

Walter F. Char, M.D.

Motivations for intercultural marriages are numerous and include most of the reasons for any marriage. In speaking of motives one must appreciate that the conscious reason given for a mixed cultural marriage might not be the actual one and that it is often the result of a combination of several factors, conscious and unconscious.

Intercultural marriages must be interpreted in the context of time, place and cultural groups involved. At present, in the melting pot of Hawaii, about 50 percent of the marriages are intercultural in nature. A marriage between a Chinese and Japanese in Hawaii is so commonplace that not much thought is given to it, whereas, a marriage between a black and Caucasian in a small hamlet in the deep South would probably be a much more serious matter. Period of time also is a factor that influences the frequency of mixed marriages. In 1974, 32 percent of all Jews in the U.S. were married to non-Jews, whereas, a decade ago only 17.4 percent were in this category.

For a marriage to take place, the motive of one partner to marry usually complements that of the other. For example, in a sadomasochistic marriage, one partner must be predominantly the sadist and the other the masochist.

Different workers use different labels to describe similar motives; therefore, the number of motives may depend on one's definition of a motive, with the motives given often overlapping one another. In addition, the list of motives given will reflect the school of thought which the worker represents. The psychoanalyst will employ concepts such as oedipal conflict in explaining motivations while the sociologist will describe it in terms such as downward and upward mobility.

Like all marriages, intercultural marriages can either be legalized marriages or common-law marriages. In this chapter, when the word marriage is mentioned, it will be used in the context of a formal, legalized marriage. Some of the motives given for intercultural marriages follow herewith.

Love as a Motive

To marry for love, especially in the West, is a highly valued motivation for marriage although it is difficult to define what love is. Is love based on a passionate, erotic attraction? Is it related to altruistic surrender of one's self to another? Is love based on companionship or on the ethics of mutually satisfying each other's needs? Partners in an intercultural marriage often mention love as the force that motivated them to get married despite severe social and family pressures against it. Lawrence Kubie, a noted psychiatrist, warns the "love" is a poor criterion for marriage since it impairs judgment in choosing a mate for a satisfactory marriage. This certainly seems true in many intercultural marriages when the involved partners get married despite the great obstacles that stand in their way of having a successful union. Yet, on the other hand, without the "glue" of love to hold things together it is doubtful that a mutually satisfying marriage can continue for long in many mixed marriages because of the many inherent problems that can cause disharmony.

Chance and Availability

Chance and availability are very important factors in the process of mate selection. This is true in all marriages but is probably more so in intercultural marriages. For example, a white American soldier stationed in Vietnam may marry a Vietnamese girl simply because of the factor of availability and propinquity in a setting where it seems appropriate. If he were not a lonely GI stationed in Vietnam for a year, he would never have an exogamous marriage. In the same way, a Chinese scholar would not have married a French girl if he was not abroad in France to study. Or, an American student from Iowa would not have married his Pakistani wife if they did not meet as fellow students at the East-West Center of Hawaii.

The Need to be Different

Our behavior is always a reflection of our individual personality and psychology. There are some who are more adventuresome than others and are always interested in trying and liking something different than the usual choice. They are always eager to try new foods or to meet new people. With this predisposition, they are much more apt to marry someone outside of their cultural background than someone with traditional choices.

An extreme of this need to be different is exhibitionism. A narcissistic, exhibitionistic person may marry outside of his race in order to be different and to attract attention. This is one of the reasons given why people from the stage and screen seem to have a higher incidence of mixed marriages.

Practical Reasons

The motives for marriage are multiple. Some may marry for love and others for strictly practical reasons. A poor, white, German girl may consent to marry a Negro soldier stationed in post war Germany for the material benefits he can give her, and the opportunity to escape from her unhappy home and come to America. Likewise, on the other side of the world, a Japanese girl might marry an American GI for similar reasons. The marriage will often break down when they return to the U.S. and she, living in an alien culture, suddenly finds that he is not only not rich but actually poor by comparison with other Americans.

Some people marry to improve their social status. A white nurse may marry an oriental physician because she thinks she will improve her social status by becoming a physician's wife. In turn the physician may see himself gaining a wife from the more highly "valued" white group. In a very early study done in Boston on black-white marriages (1914-1935), Worth and Goldhammer found that the negro men had superior occupational positions than did their white brides. This might not hold true today where conditions are different and other motives may be more important.

Problems Related to "Oedipus Complex"

Many psychiatrists, particularly the psychoanalyst, believe that the phenomenon of exogamy or intercultural marriage is strongly rooted in the phenomenon of the "Oedipus complex." According to the psychoanalytic theory of child development, around the age of three to five a child begins to develop intense positive feelings toward the parent of the opposite sex. Associated with this is the development of strong negative feelings toward the parent of the same sex, whom he sees as a competitor for the affection of the parent of the opposite sex, thus creating a so-called triangular conflict. Normally, the child overcomes this conflict by identifying with the parent of his own sex and becomes interested in heterosexual objects other than his own opposite-sex parent. However for various reasons, a child may not be able to resolve his oedipal conflict successfully, and this will influence his choice of mate late on in life. According to the well-known psychoanalyst Karl Abraham, one of the ways to cope with this unresolved oedipal conflict is to choose a special type of mate for marriage. In an early paper, he contrasted marriage between close relatives with mixed marriage. He stated that the former represents a pathological oedipal fixation, while the latter constitutes an "Exaggerated Phobia of Incest." This means that if a child was strongly attached to his parent of the opposite sex he might later choose a close relative, such as his cousin who closely resembles his own parent of the opposite sex, for his wife. However, if he is phobic of incest, he is then driven to choose a mate who is very different from his own opposite sex parent. For example, a Jewish male who was extremely close to his mother might then go out of his way to marry a black girl as a defense against his incestuous fears.

What resulted as a defense against incest may also happen for different motives. An individual may have such negative feelings toward the parent of the opposite sex that he or she must find a spouse completely different from that parent, a love object of another color. Also, an individual out of feelings of fear, guilt, or inadequacy about competition with the parent of the same sex for the affection of someone like the opposite-sex parent, circumvents this competition by finding a mate outside his race.

The family problem may also extend to other members of the family such as a sibling. Therefore, incest fears or strong negative reactions toward a sibling of the opposite sex may influence an individual to choose a mate very different from that sibling.

Another example of how a person's early childhood and love objects may later influence his choice of a mate deals with the concept of fixation on an early infantile love object. It has been theorized that when (if) a white Southern heiress runs off and marries her black chauffeur, it might be due to the fact that when she was young, she was cared for by a beloved black mammy and played with her children. Her marriage to her black chauffeur is her return to an early love object.

36

Messages Given by Parents

If a parent is not satisfied with his own spouse, he may consciously or unconsciously encourage his children to marry someone who is very different from his own spouse. For example, a Japanese mother might tell her daughter to look for a Chinese husband because he will be more helpful around the house and not simply expect to be waited upon, like her father. Or a Hawaiian father might tell his son to look for a Japanese wife because she will be thrifty and help him save money, unlike his mother. Often the message might not be given so explicitly but more by innuendo.

The opposite can also happen. An individual's parents may strongly insist that he or she marry someone within their own ethnic group. Out of rebellion, the individual might do the opposite and marry someone very much outside their group.

Beliefs about Other Cultures

People have beliefs about their culture and other cultures which may or may not be founded on reality. Based on such beliefs, an intercultural marriage may result. There are some who say that they married someone from another culture because that person possesses a valued attribute that their own culture is not as likely to supply. For example, a white male might marry a Japanese woman because he feels a Japanese female can better satisfy his desire to have a wife who is willing to wait on him. A Hawaiian woman on the other hand might marry a Chinese male because she believes that a Chinese husband is more apt to give her financial security than someone from her own groups.

Sexual fantasies also contribute to the making of intercultural marriages. The sexual basis for intercultural marriages is often based on stereotypical fantasy rather than reality. Negro men are reputed to be more virile and Negro women to be more sexually passionate. A Japanese female's role in life is supposed to be to please her husband. Therefore, a white male who feels sexually inadequate with white females whom he sees as being very demanding and contrasting might deliberately seek a Japanese mate as a sexual object. A Jewish male who neurotically sees his mother as a pure madonna and can function sexually only with a devalued woman, may seek a nonwhite, "sexy" female for a mate. Exotic can become erotic and the lure of the "forbidden fruit" is very strong especially if the individual is not comfortable with his or her own sexuality.

Feelings of Superiority and Inferiority

Although often consciously denied, there is a strong tendency for people to rank races, ethnic groups and cultures as being superior or inferior to one another. This concept of superiority and inferiority can act as a motivating factor in intercultural marriages. First, let us deal with the concept of inferiority. An individual with a handicap (physically, socially, or mentally) may feel he can find acceptance only by a member of a less "valued" cultural group. A Caucasian male, for example, who is crippled by polio might marry a Puerto Rican girl who is less educated than he is, but whom he feels accepts his handicap. This sense of inferiority and inadequacy may not be based on reality but is psychologically produced and perpetuated (neurotic feelings of being physically unattractive, socially inadequate, and so on). Nevertheless, this sense of inferiority may force the individual to feel that he can find acceptance and feel adequate only with a less "valued" object, and by his belief and behavior it may well work out that way in reality.

Related to the concept of inferiority, some people may marry interculturally as a stand-in marriage or second best marriage. A man or woman may marry outside his or her race on a second best basis. A woman with a child born out of wedlock, for example, would prefer to marry someone in her group. But because she has a child to support she would marry someone outside her ethnic group, usually a member of a less "valued" group, because he is the only one that is willing to marry her and support her child. Hugo Geigel quotes Joseph Golden's 1953 study on interracial marriages in Philadelphia, which shows that one-fourth of the white brides of black men were divorcees with a higher median age than the average bride.

On the other side of the coin is the concept of superiority and the need to rescue someone of an "inferior" cultural group. For example, an American missionary working in Korea may marry an uneducated Korean woman in order to rescue her from what he thinks is her unhappy and heathen life.

Act of Aggression toward Another Race

A black male angry at whites may marry a white female as an act of defiance and revenge against the whites; the fear of many Southern whites is that all blacks covet their daughters and their greatest humiliation is for their daughters to marry blacks. Of course, in this circumstance there is often a complementary need for the white female to feel inferior about herself, or feel angry toward her own parents and culture so that her marriage with the black male is an act of rebellion against parents and society.

"Idealistic" Act

A "liberal" with high ideals regarding race relationships and the equality of man may marry someone outside his or her race as a result of those ideals. Unconsciously this action might be based on such motives as a rescue fantasy, identification with the underdog, rebellion against authority, or an inferiority complex. A study has shown that liberal, Jewish girls are over represented in intercultural marriages as compared with the rest of the population. The success of the "Black is Beautiful" movement has also changed things so that "value" of blacks have been much increased, and in fact to marry a black in some liberal circles might be a status symbol.

Sadomasochistic Reasons

Not all marriages are based on love. There are many sadomasochistic marriages. A white male may marry a black "slave" whom he can control and hurt. A black male may marry a white "slave" whom he can tease and humiliate knowing that she cannot escape from him because she has alienated herself from her family and friends by marrying him.

An individual, out of his masochistic needs, may get himself into a destructive intercultural marriage which he cannot escape from because of this masochism. At times the results of such unions are so appalling that it can almost be interpreted as a form of social suicide.

There are two extreme views regarding intercultural marriages. One is to see them as an idealistic, progressive form of human relationships where prejudices and biases are broken down, and the individuals who participate in them as strong, courageous, and idealistic. The other point of view is to see most intercultural marriages as basically unwholesome, and those who take part in them as unwise or maladjusted.

Depending on how one feels about intercultural marriages, one will tend to see motivations for intercultural marriages as being positive or negative. Many motives for intercultural marriages were enumerated in the above. In reviewing them, it seems that most could be interpreted as being negative but it was not purposely meant to express them that way. As stated in the introductory paragraph, almost all the motives given for all marriages can be considered as being the basis for intercultural marriages also. The list of above motives contains additional ones that are more specifically related to intercultural marriages. When the unconscious is studied and the motives of people are examined coldly and deeply, one can come out with an uncomfortable feeling that everyone is unhealthy and neurotic if one chooses to see it that way. But experienced clinicians, in analyzing behavior of people and including their own motivational pattern, try to uncover what is happening and why it is happening without putting a value judgment on it.

REFERENCES

Bateson, G. Redundancy and coduig. In *Steps to an Ecology of Mind.* New York: Chanceller Publishing Co., 1972.

Beigel, H. Problems and motives in interracial relationships. *Journal of Sex Research* 2:185-205, 1966.

Berelson, B. and Steiner, G. *Human Behavior.* New York: Harcourt, Brace and World, 1964.

Birdwhistell, R. *Kinesics and Context.* New York: Ballantine Books, 1972.

Calkins, F. *My Samoan Chief.* New York: Doubleday and Co., 1962.

Lehrman, S. Psychopathology in mixed marriages. *Psychoanalytic Quarterly* 36:67-82, 1967.

Little, G. Analytic reflections on mixed marriages. *Psychoanalytic Review* 29:20-25, 1942.

Saucher, J. F. Psychodynamics of interethnic marriage. *Canadian Psychiatric Association Journal* 15:129-134, 1970.

Shapiro, H. L. *The Heritage of the Bounty,* New York: Simon and Schuster, 1936.

5

Intercultural Marriage in Hawaii

Kenneth O. Sanborn, Ph.D.

Intercultural marriage, between partners of different cultural traditions, grows increasingly common in Hawaii. Romanzo Adams, a pioneer in the study of interethnic marriage in Hawaii, began a literature on the subject with his book, *Interracial Marriage*. His pioneer work has been supplemented by a number of studies through the years that have increased our knowledge of some of the social factors that contribute to the phenomenon. Interethnic divorce has been considered as well.

Social Factors

Although new information has increased our understanding of this social process, it has not been very significant in helping the mental health profession deal with intercultural marriage problems.

In this chapter, we review some past studies focused on Hawaii, some related studies from outside Hawaii, and some recent data that increase our knowledge of cultural fusion and provide the groundwork for studying some of the specific cultural stresses that affect persons who have chosen to live their lives with someone from a different tradition.

Adams categorized ethnic groups on the basis of organization. For example, he described Orientals as members of cultures with strict rules, regulations, and expectations that resulted in a more organized approach to life. Hawaiians and part-Hawaiians were seen as members of a culture with fewer organizational restraints on their behavior than the Japanese or the Chinese.

He predicted that less organized groups would show both more out-marriage and more divorce, while organized groups would have the lowest percentages of out-marriage and divorce because of their more effective social control. Should a person from a less organized group marry someone from an organized group, Adams predicted an averaging effect on the out-marriage and divorce rate. Marriage between members of two well organized groups, on the other hand, would be as enduring as an in-marriage in either group.

Adam's thesis has been difficult to test because the concept of organization is not well defined and measured. Any index which varies widely within an ethnic group makes group comparisons less significant. Some organized groups have been found to show higher divorce rates than less organized groups, disproving the generality of Adams' thesis.

For five of the groups, Hawaiian, Korean, Puerto Rican, Filipino, and Caucasian, Andrew Lind (1964), one of Adams' foremost students, demonstrated that out-marriages had fewer divorces than in-marriages. This is shown in Table 1. By Adams' thesis this could be true only if the in-marriages were with partners from more organized groups. Japanese and part-Hawaiian combinations have low percentages of divorce. Caucasian husbands clearly fare better with Puerto Rican or Filipino wives with rates of 20.1 and 24.4. Divorce rates for in-marriages in both these groups are nearly twice as high.

According to Lind, the size of an ethnic group has a major effect on the number of out-marriages; in the larger groups, out-marriages are proportionately fewer. Lind attributes this fact to the presence of more effective "moral control" over the members of larger groups than is present in the smaller groups. If this is true, then in-marriages in small

Table 1: Interracial Marriage and Divorce Rate (from Lind, A. W., 1964)

Ethnic group	Out-marriage rate (1956-1960) per 100 marriages	Divorces (1958-1962) per 100 marriages		
		In-	Out-	Both
Hawaiian	85	55	38*	41
Korean	77	57	36*	41
Puerto Rican	61	46	27*	34
Part-Hawaiian	52	22	27	26
Chinese	49	18	25	21
Filipino	46	46	28*	38
Black	46	34	36	35
Caucasian	31	35	31*	34
Japanese	17	15	27	17
Total population	39	27	29	28

*Out-marriage divorce rate is less than in-marriage divorce rate.

groups could represent cases of higher risk for divorce. Lack of sufficient numbers to exert moral control could result in both high out-marriage rate and high in-marriage divorce rate. The concept of "moral control" has the same measurement problems as Adams' idea of organization.

The Filipinos are often described as a group with special conditions that stem from the peculiar circumstances of their immigration. They came to Hawaii without wives, resulting in the highest ratio of men to women on the plantations. After living in Hawaii a number of years, many had saved enough money to marry young wives from the Philippines. Some of these marriages may have been unstable due to the large age difference between the spouses.

A variety of social circumstances, according to Lind, have differentially affected the other groups. Recency of arrival, sex balance within the group, existence of ethnocentric versus permissive family traditions, and the secularizing influences of urbanized life all appear to play a role in the interethnic out-marriage and divorce trends in Hawaii.

Robert Schmidt (1967), the state statistician, brought attention to the relationship of interethnic marriage and social class. He found white collar males to be far less likely than blue collar males to marry outside their own ethnic group except for Hawaiians and part-Hawaiians. He also found that the number of interracial marriages was higher per capita in rural Hawaii, for brides under twenty, for couples in operative, service, or laborer occupations, and for couples with lower than median incomes.

Clarence Glick (1972), a researcher at the University of Hawaii, found that 11 percent of inter-marriages in the 1960s were Asian-Asian; while 43 percent were Asian—non-Asian marriages. Three fourths of the children of in-marriage in Hawaii have some Hawaiian ancestry. Glick went on to determine that the smaller ethnic groups, such as Korean or Puerto Rican, show higher out-marriage rates for females than do the larger groups. Groups that have been in the islands longer, such as Chinese or Portuguese, tend to have higher out-marriage rates. Those with a shorter history, Japanese and Filipinos as examples, respond more to tradition and marry within their own group.

The actual number of intercultural marriages of various crosses for the decade 1960 to 1969 is also described by Glick. He suggests that there are natural forces such as those suggested by Lind that effect intermarriage in Hawaii.

The number of out-marriages during this decade is shown in Table 2. Caucasian and part-Hawaiian combinations represent about half of the total.

Ch'eng K'un Cheng and Douglas Yamamura (1957), two researchers

Table 2: Ethnicity of Spouses in Out-Marriage from 1960 to 1969

Wife	Husband	No. of marriages
Part-Hawaiian	Caucasian	3,006
Caucasian	Part-Hawaiian	2,031
Japanese	Caucasian	1,660
Filipino	Caucasian	1,422
Part-Hawaiian	Filipino	1,000 plus
Japanese	Part-Hawaiian	1,000 plus

at the University of Hawaii, published the 1950 statistics on the number of men in each ethnic group for each woman: Filipino, 2.5; Caucasian, 1.3; Korean, 1.2; Chinese and Puerto Rican, 1.1; with Japanese almost equally balanced between men and women. Out-marriages between part-Hawaiian women and non-Hawaiian men before 1945 is determined, in part, by the length of contact, the degree of economic well-being and the sex ratios of the non-Hawaiian groups.

They point out that women in ethnic groups with a balanced sex ratio, such as the Japanese, tend to marry out of their group more than women in a group with a larger number of men than women. The percentage by sex who have married out is shown in Table 3.

Compatible Cultural Backgrounds

Both men and women tend to marry persons whose cultural and ethnic backgrounds are similar to their own, although some women who marry out marry into a higher social class.

Margaret Parkman and Jack Sawyer (1964), two researchers using a statistical approach, followed up earlier studies on the way in which "like marries like." They found that members of ethnic groups out-marry more with members of other ethnic groups who have backgrounds similar in cultural tradition and similar in adaptation to contemporary urban society. These two factors, called East/west and urbanism, account for 77 percent of the variance in the study.

The East/west dimension reflects a combination of characteristics including race, religion, and nationality. The dimension begins at one extreme with Japanese and continues through Korean, Chinese, Hawaiian, part-Hawaiian, Caucasian, Filipino, to Puerto Rican at the other extreme. The dimension appears to distinguish between groups whose tradition is Buddhist and those with a Christian tradition. The more similar two groups are in cultural background, the more likely their members are to intermarry.

44

Table 3: Percentage of Each Sex that Out-Marry in Each Ethnic Group

Ethnic group	% Women	% Men
Japanese	78	22
Part-Hawaiian	69	31
Puerto Rican	63	37
Korean	59	41
Chinese	54	46
Filipino	36	62
Caucasian	21	79

Urbanism is defined as the proportion of an ethnic group's population living in Honolulu as compared to the rest of Hawaii. Proximity is not the issue here. Rather, the amount of urbanism in the culture, is. They describe urbanism as intensified mobility, flexibility in social structures, and differential participation in groups with a high rate of turnover. Moving to the city signals a shift from traditional to modern values throughout the ethnic group.

Cultural Styles

Now let us consider certain marriages based on two large groupings of lifestyle: traditional and modern. In this case, traditional marriage and contemporary marriage.

Traditional conceptions of marriage arise out of earlier, agrarian times. The traditional family's basic functions were mutual security, procreation, and child rearing, as well as other economic, religious, and emotional needs. While norms varied from culture to culture, roles were generally fixed and well defined, and families functioned as both economic and territorial units. Violations of taboos and mores were rare and when they occurred often seemed influenced by psychopathological factors.

Relationships between persons in a traditional society were often "complementary." That is, when men were dominant, women tended to be more submissive; when parents were nurturant, children were succorant. The complementarity served to keep roles fixed and the society stable.

Modern urban society, on the other hand, may be more often described as "symmetrical." When a husband expresses anger toward his wife, she is quite likely to express anger back. When parents are quiet, the children may be quiet also.

When we look at intermarriage as representing a combination of the two cultural styles, complementary and symmetrical, we can generate a typology of four possible marriage types within a culture: (1) complementary: husband dominant; (2) complementary: wife dominant; (3) symmetrical: partners autonomous; (4) symmetrical: partners syncretic. Autonomous signifies that each goes his own way; syncretic means going together.

Two of the four types of marriage have been studied by Robert Blood, a leading sociologist in the study of marital adjustment, in *Love Match or Arranged Marriage: A Tokyo—Detroit Comparison* (1962), in which he described the repercussions of the various interaction patterns. The study points to behaviors that need to be related to intercultural marriage. The behaviors are more observable than single hypothetical concepts such as Adams' "organization" or Lind's "moral control." They can provide a deeper level of analysis than statistical indices of divorce.

The first measure is the power structure of the family, or who makes decisions about what; second, the division of labor in the home; third, courtesy as expressed in precedence patterns and giving appreciation; fourth, companionship including internal communication and external sociability; fifth, therapeutic interdependence; and finally sixth, expression of affection and sexual activity all may be considered in a description of marital adjustment. Using measures taken from the above areas, Blood has found that these areas can distinguish between the behavior of different types of marriage within a culture, for example, the "love match" and the "arranged marriage" in Japan. His methods have yet to be tried with traditional and modern intercultural marriage types found in Hawaii.

Ari Kiev, a well-known transcultural psychiatrist, considered the possible outcomes of two types of intercultural marriage; the traditional wife marrying the modern husband, the modern wife marrying the traditional husband. Taboos against various forms of intermarriage are strongest in traditional societies where role relationships are fixed and well defined and the family functions as an economic and territorial unit.

Where there are traditions, violations of a taboo are more likely to be influenced by individual psychopathology than by healthy responses to changing social conditions. Social change leads to increasing unfamiliarity with traditional norms and to a search for new norms to meet present conditions. Intermarriages that work overseas may fall apart at home, then improve again in a move to a setting that can accept differences in partners. Many intermarried couples move to Hawaii for this reason.

In the early stages of intermarriage, the major problems relate to the responses of the community and to the families of the two partners. In later stages, the marriage undergoes the normal internal strains of married life. These strains may be intensified by the cultural differences of the partners. Kiev presents two scenarios of intercultural marriage.

46

Scenario one (traditional wife, modern husband). A wife from a traditional culture may have learned some of the following behaviors: to support patriarchal values, to defer to male authority, to be supportive and nurturing to men, to orient her life around the home, to underplay individual motives, to meet the traditional obligations of her group, to support the dependency needs of her husband.

These behaviors may appeal to certain husbands from a modern tradition who respond with the following behaviors: to show paternalistic concern for his wife, to be protective of her welfare, to act as if he were "the lord of the manor."

The couple's life proceeds amicably until the first child is born. Then the following behaviors may occur: the wife turns her main attention to the child, the husband feels rejected, he tries to overcome these feelings by showing interest in other women and spending more time with friends. The absence of the husband's presence and his emotional support plus the absence of the extended families' support may lead to the wife developing symptoms, often of depression.

Scenario two (the modern wife, traditional husband). A husband from a traditional ethnic group may have adapted to and not be aware of his own dependency needs or his need to be treated deferentially. He may appear to his modern wife to be over-involved with his family. He turns to his mother for support and defers to his father in making decisions. He does not feel adequate to deal with a large variety of role relationships outside of his cultural milieu. He may have strong feelings of jealousy about his wife and her male friends.

The modern wife is attractive to her traditional husband because of her apparent independence. On the other hand, she may be unwilling to cater to the dependency needs of her children and tries to encourage independent behaviors similar to her own. She may limit the number of children she has. She values a sense of freedom and may feel that her husband, while attractive and courtly, may be tying her down. She easily establishes relationships in her own world that can appear too familiar to her husband.

Crisis situations such as these may be difficult to resolve. The parties involved do not see the basic unconscious values and attitudes that are contributing. Traditional societies define more rigidly the roles of men and women, place greater emphasis on the prerogatives of age, the preservation of the status quo, the inequality of sexes, the prerogatives of men, the constraints on women, and the significance of inherited versus achieved status. If they do indeed produce "complementary" relationships, each member may learn that dominance begets submission and submission begets dominance.

In "symmetrical" or more modern societies, dominance usually begets dominance and submission begets submission. One's strategy, unconscious or otherwise, must vary according to his or her background. Under stress one usually reverts to his or her earlier learning so that problems of early cultural learning may only arise during periods of family stress.

These are at least two major cultural traditions in Honolulu: traditional and modern, both of which include Oriental, Polynesian and European peoples. The length of residence of the family in Hawaii is related to their degree of modernity.

As intermarriage increases, it produces a third culture of persons who have learned to deal with cultural differences. This new group is a significant part of the population of Hawaii and assumes many of the characteristics of a new ethnic group. Its behavior develops in response to the requirements of the local situation, which includes several ethnic traditions and many more marital mixes in which the partners have similar problems that they can share with others.

The sexes in each ethnic group differ in their emotional behavior in relation to each other. Chinese women are more emotionally expressive than Chinese men, while Filipino men are more expressive than Filipino women. How that relates in the combinations of intercultural marriage has only recently begun to be explored.

Divorce Rates

By looking at divorce rates by ethnic group and marital role, we may be able to learn something of the relative stress and strain internal to intercultural marriage.

Table 4 is taken from Lind's data for 1958 through 1962. It shows the divorce rate (number of divorces per 100 population) for in-marriages in five ethnic groups. The other numbers are the predicted out-marriage divorce rates arrived at by averaging two in-marriage rates. Table 5 shows the actual rates for the out-marriage combinations for the period. Table 6 roughly indicates whether actual divorce rates were above (+) or below (−) the predicted rates.

In general, the Chinese man has higher divorce rates than expected, as does the Caucasian woman. These differences can possibly be explained by norms of emotional difference between the sexes in each ethnic group.

The most divorce-prone combinations involve Caucasian women married to Japanese or Chinese men whose ethnic groups normally have the lowest divorce rates in Hawaii. Perhaps, as Blood theorizes (1969), the very stability of these groups is the source of trouble. Apparently the same solidarity of family structure which oppresses Oriental, emancipation-seeking women also annoys the already emancipated Caucasian woman. The Japanese or Chinese husbands and their extended families may have sought to assert their traditional authority over these wives without success. A Caucasian wife may be too assertive to submit to

Table 4: Predicted Divorce Rates for Five Ethnic Groups
(1958–1962)

Husband	Wife				
	Chinese	Caucasian	Hawaiian	Japanese	Filipino
Chinese	18	27	20	17	32
Caucasian	27	35	29	25	41
Hawaiian	20	29	22	19	34
Japanese	17	25	19	15	31
Filipino	32	41	34	31	46

Table 5: Actual Divorce Rates for Five Ethnic Groups
(1958–1962)

Husband	Wife				
	Chinese	Caucasian	Hawaiian	Japanese	Filipino
Chinese	18	43	32	16	*
Caucasian	31	35	26	31	24
Hawaiian	24	35	22	28	21
Japanese	14	58	20	15	20
Filipino	*	43	27	26	46

*No data available on this marriage combination.

Table 6: Outcome Differences between the Predicted and the
Actual Divorce Rates (1958–1962)

Husband	Wife				
	Chinese	Caucasian	Hawaiian	Japanese	Filipino
Chinese	0	++	++	0	*
Caucasian	0	0	0	++	——
Hawaiian	0	++	0	++	——
Japanese	0	++	0	0	——
Filipino	*	0	——	——	0

++ = Actual divorce rate exceeds predicted divorce rate.
—— = Predicted divorce rate exceeds actual divorce rate.
*No data available on this marriage combination.

patriarchy and would rather get a divorce. Caught in a power struggle with a domineering husband and family, a wife accustomed to equality may want out.

At the opposite extreme, the least divorce-prone marriages in Hawaii paired Caucasian men with Puerto Rican or Filipino women, where the converse situation exists. Caucasian men may be accustomed to equality but women from Spanish cultures are often more submissive. More importantly perhaps, the relatively low status of their island economies probably encourages the wife to look up to her Caucasian husband and feel grateful to and dependent on him. For her this is an unusually "good" marriage which she would be reluctant to leave. Such marriages are not necessarily the most satisfying. They may be deficient in companionship and empathy, but they are extraordinarily stable.

REFERENCES

Adams, R. *Interracial Marriage in Hawaii*. New York: Macmillan Co., 1937.

Bateson, G. *Steps to an Ecology of Mind*. San Francisco: Chandler Publishing Co., 1972.

Bloos, R. O., Jr. *Love Match or Arranged Marriage: A Tokyo-Detroit Comparison*. New York: Free Press, 1967.

Blood, R. O., Jr. *Marriage*. New YOrk: Free Press, 1969.

Ch'eng, C. K. and Yamamura, D. S. Interracial marriage and divorce in Hawaii. *Social Forces* 36:77-84, 1957.

Glick, C. E. Interracial marriage and admixture in Hawaii. *Social Biology* 17:278-291, 1972.

Lind, A. W. Interracial marriage as affecting divorce in Hawaii. *Sociology and Social Research* 49:17-26, 1964.

Parkman, M. A. and Sawyer, J. Dimensions of intermarriage in Hawaii. *American Sociological Review* 32:593-607, 1967.

Schmitt, R. C. Interracial households and family income differentials. *Sociology and Social Research* 46(2):203-206, 1962.

6
Intercultural Marriage: Problem Areas

Richard Markoff, M.D.

Within any particular culture, marriage has its own special liabilities and problems, and particular marriages succeed or fail to different degrees. This is true even for cultures in which divorce does not occur as frequently as in the United States and Western Europe: the integrity of a marriage, after all, is only one dimension of success.

Factors of many sorts—personal, social, physical, economic—may interact to shape and generate problems in any marriage. However, there are other factors which may have special relevance for intercultural marriage. These influences tend to be greatest when we deal with substantially dissimilar, internally homogeneous cultures. The main business of this chapter will be to examine some of the special factors and special problem areas which are peculiarly relevant to success or failure in intercultural marriage; although, from what has been said above, it should be clear that they do not by themselves predict the success or failure of any given intercultural marriage.

Problems in Communication

Marriage demands that partners communicate their thoughts and feelings to one another, and the first of the major problem areas for intercultural marriage is that of communication. On first mention of communication, one tends to think of language, although this most obvious channel of communication is not the one which is most significant for marriage. Nevertheless, there are some aspects of language which are highly important, for while language is the clearest channel of communication, it may contain ambiguities which represent a source of difficulty. Take, for example, the following brief dialogue:

Husband: I think we should visit my sister this weekend.

Wife: Yes.

Clearly, there are ambiguities here. Is the husband's statement exactly what it seems to be—statement of opinion? Or is it perhaps a request, or even a demand? Does the wife's "yes" indicate that she too thinks that they should visit her sister-in-law, or does it merely recognize her husband's opinion that they should do so? Does it signify acquiescence, without necessarily meaning agreement, as does the "yes, sir" response to a military command?

The unclarity becomes compounded when different cultures use the same word to serve different functions. Thus, in cultures (for example, the traditional Chinese) which place great importance upon maintaining a smooth, unruffled flow of interpersonal face-to-face relations, there may be many subtle and delicate differences in the way apparent agreement is expressed; and these shades and nuances of agreement may actually express, or allow room for, a considerable amount of disagreement. Such a culture may reserve the expression "no" for differences which are total and cannot be reconciled. On the contrary, other cultures may use "No" freely even in cases of mild and temporary disagreement, and an individual from such a culture may be strikingly obtuse to the varieties of meaning that can be encoded in expressions of agreement. If we apply the above specimen of dialogue to an intercultural marriage in which "yes" and "no" have these differing significances, we clearly have a situation which might be productive of very considerable conflict. To the husband coming, say, from a culture in which "no" is used freely, the wife's "yes" might signify cheerful and ready agreement; while the wife coming from a culture which uses "no" only for extreme situations, might actually be expressing reluctance. (Had the wife really meant what the husband thought she meant, her "yes" might have been accompanied by a set of reinforcing phrases, or by nonverbal modifiers.)

The verbal expression of thanks offers another illustration of this sort of problem. In Japanese culture, such verbal expressions are confined to situations that call for some degree of formality and would tend not to be used within the family. In Western society, the verbal "thank you" is used freely and frequently in all situations, both formal and informal, and might well be expected between members of the family. An American wife might be hurt by her husband's omission of verbal thanks for a birthday gift, while a Japanese wife might well be puzzled and wonder why she was being treated as a stranger, if her husband did thank her.

Beyond the main body of basic, relatively stable language lies the realm of colloquialisms. These are constantly changing and often draw both their content and form from recent events and trends within a particular culture or community. Ignorance of this language, and more generally, the absence of a repertoire of shared ideas and experience may impede communication within an intercultural marriage.

While language can thus lead to some difficulties in communication, it is probably not the most important source of such difficulties. Most intercultural couples probably learn fairly readily to take into account differences in the use of words. In fact, one may suppose that difficulties such as this would arise mainly where the two native languages were fairly closely related, or where the common language of the marriage was spoken with proficiency by both partners. The more obvious the language barrier, the more it would be likely to be taken in account.

Of greater significance, probably, is the area of nonverbal communication. This is a very large area, and includes facial expression, gesture and dress; the way people position themselves with respect to one another in a conversation or other social interaction; vocal inflection; and kind and degree of physical contact. The major reason for the importance of nonverbal communication is that it is used, perhaps to a greater degree than verbal communication, to express feelings and emotional responses. Gregory Bateson has suggested that nonverbal "languages" are specifically and characteristically used to communicate about interpersonal relationships, rather than merely to embellish verbal interchange. Also, nonverbal communications tend to be less well defined than verbal languages, and contain space for greater ambiguity. Finally, less explicit attention is usually paid to nonverbal than to verbal communication skills, while the broad range of behavior included within nonverbal communication makes it a difficult repertoire to master.

Some cultures—the American, for example—tend not to specify or emphasize nonverbal communication. A person from such a culture may take such matters for granted. Such a person may be perfectly aware even of the subtler sorts of linguistic difference while neglecting crucial differences in styles of nonverbal communication. Conflicts may arise which then appear to be inexplicable and lead to considerable discord. This individual who is unintentionally deceived through his failure to decode nonverbal communication will generally be sincerely puzzled and indignant. He may also feel helpless because of his inability to pinpoint the source of the difficulty.

As an example of confusion in nonverbal communication, consider the exchange of greetings. In Japan, the custom of bowing is a highly developed system, delicately attuned to social status and reflecting recognition of very specific status differences. A continuum of expression rang-ing from very deep respect to open and sarcastic disrespect can be expressed. How deeply one bows, how many times, and who bows first convey specific meaning in Japanese culture. Foreigners may easily, and quite inadvertently, misuse this system of communication with highly undesirable effect. Americans, on the other hand, utilize a considerable variety of greeting gestures. Imagine the confusion of a Chinese im-migrant greeting his American mother-in-law for the first time. He has seen Americans shake hands, hug each other, kiss cheeks, kiss lips, or simply nod or smile. The choice of a correct and acceptable behavior may well be difficult to make.

Cultures differ not only in the meanings attached to particular postures, gestures and the like, but also in more general aspects that may be described as the "style" of nonverbal communication. Thus, we have the characteristic style of the English, who combine linguistic un-derstatement with a highly controlled and restricted use of gesture. In contrast, there is the free and expansive gestural language of the Italians and the French. Such stylistic differences lend themselves particularly to misinterpretation of the amount of feeling which is being expressed. Other distinctions of nonverbal style involve the use made of various channels of expression. Facial expression may be exploited heavily in nonverbal communication in one culture, while hand gestures play a highly significant role in another.

Finally, there are nonverbal communications which are mediated by the degree and patterning of physical proximity, and by touch. Obvious-ly, these are components of nonverbal communication in which cultures differ sharply. There are cultures, such as that of Samoa, which use physical contact quite extensively as a means of expression in a variety of situations and with many meanings. Other cultures—again, the English may be cited—utilize restricted and stylized physical contact. Per-sons from cultures patterned after this latter fashion are more likely to at-tach sexual or aggressive meaning to attempts at communication by physical contact.

The reader is advised to consult the works of Birdwhistell such as "Kinesics and Context" for further information on communication through "body language."

Differences in Values

Cultures differ widely in their value systems. Despite recent trends, the acquisition of material wealth, competitive success, and upward social movement remain important values for a great many North Americans. In contrast, in Polynesian cultures, individual striving for material success often has a lower value than the maintenance of cooperative and mutually interdependent relationships within the family group and within the larger Polynesian community. In the traditional cultures of Japan and China, dignity, and the regard and esteem of others is a highly important value; while in Occidental cultures, independence in thought and action is especially valued.

Cultures are not monolithic as regards value systems, and often—characteristically perhaps—there are different and even conflicting values within any given society. Not only does each culture contain sub-cultures, but there are "ideal" values, seldom realized in practice; and there are the everyday values that are less often explicitly stated than embodied in common social actions. Given such complexity, it is not surprising that differences in values may lead to considerable conflict in the intercultural marriage.

What makes the area of values so important a source of problems is not merely that cultures differ in their value systems, but that all of us tend to feel that our particular culturally ordained values are incontestably "right" or "true" or "the best." This quality of essential rightness is inherent in value systems, for each culture tends to teach its particular value system as representing the most appropriate way to conduct one's life. It is very difficult even for the most highly educated and cosmopolitan members of a culture to accept fully the validity of value systems contrary to those with which they were brought up. Frequently, an acceptance of the validity of contrary value systems remains simply intellectual while on the level of feeling, one's own value system still seems "best."

Not only do value systems seem to have an essential "rightness" about them, but they tend also to be unobtrusive. We frequently do not recognize that we subscribe to a particular set of values until they are challenged—perhaps by the fact that we encounter someone from another culture, whose values differ from ours. Thus, it often comes as a shock that not everyone shares our particular values, and we may experience the same sense of disbelief, helplessness and perhaps indignation as when a nonverbal miscommunication occurs.

An especially clear illustration of value conflict may sometimes be observed in Caucasian-Polynesian marriages. Here, the North American or European values of individual striving and material success, expressed in the acquisition and personal ownership of goods, may come into conflict with the Polynesian tendency to value the welfare of the family as a community above its individual members, and to share in common certain material possessions. An instance of this is provided in Calkins' book *My Samoan Chief.* The problem here is a conflict over a material possession—in this case, a car—which the wife (Calkins) regards as belonging to herself and her husband alone, a view not shared, apparently, by her husband's Samoan relatives. A similar conflict might occur, in a Caucasian-Polynesian marriage, in terms of the extent of hospitality to be extended to a visiting family member. The Polynesian partner might expect to share his home with even a fairly distantly related person, while the Caucasian partner might well think in terms of hotel accommodations.

The Concept of Marriage

Cultures differ in the way they define marriage. Each culture, by means of a particular set of values, delineates the aims and objectives of marriage. And each culture develops its own model for the marital relationship by prescribing uniquely: the nature of the sexual relationship; the manner in which children shall be reared; the division of labor and responsibility; and the nature of love as it applies to marriage. Finally, cultures specify how and when a marital partner is to be selected and from what subgroup within the population.

One may think of these several elements as forming a concept of marriage which is unique for each culture. While the concept of marriage which a particular culture generates is not organized in a perfectly logical, internally consistent fashion, it is not merely a collection of individual descriptive and defining characteristics which just happen to have developed together, and within which no organization or structure is readily discernible. Rather, the concept of marriage is so structured that the values within it that specify the objectives and aims of marriage serve to rationalize and justify the various features of marital relationship and choice of marital partner. This should not be taken to mean that the concept of marriage develops entirely as a theoretically based piece of social engineering; it is more probable that it arises, in part, out of the need to create rational-seeming structures out of whatever is actually in being.

It is not unusual to find that different cultures have antithetical, almost mutually exclusive, concepts of marriage. The modern, Western concept of marriage, which emphasizes romantic love as a basis for selection of partner, and mutual self-realization as an important goal, is obviously in conflict with concepts of marriage that could be found in a number of Oriental cultures. These make use of "arrangement" as a method of partner selection, and introduce important economic and even political elements into the goals of marriage. Such a concept of marriage is, of course, far from exclusively Oriental. It exists elsewhere today, and it represented the dominant concept of marriage in Occidental cultures until quite recent times.

Certain cultural combinations may have a better "fit" with one another in regard to concepts of marriage than others. For example, a Chinese man marrying a Hawaiian woman may find that his concept of marriage fits fairly well with hers: both strongly value children; and both involve an extended family within which the marriage-pair occupies a specific and well-structured place. Other cultural combinations may be particularly liable to conflict. For example, Filipino culture tends to be more tolerant of infidelity on the part of husbands than is the American culture. An American wife might be greatly distressed by what her Filipino husband considered normal and permissible. His behavior might be quite discordant with her idea of marriage while being entirely consistent with his.

Autonomous Behavior and Practices

The concept of marriage, as has been stated, is not a deductively logical, internally consistent structure, in which there are always clear relationships between aims and objectives on the one hand, and particular practical arrangements and behaviors on the other. At every level, rather, there exist specific practices and arrangements which have little to do with aims and objectives; and form many specific arrangements and practices, there might be alternatives which would serve just as well.

Culture, as a totality, is similarly organized. There are broad and general consistencies to be observed in the relationship between customary practices and the material conditions of life on the one hand, and systems of values on the other. But as one sharpens one's focus and becomes more specific, many inconsistencies appear. There are practices which may once have had a clear relationship to particular necessities but which have lost that relevance. There are particular solutions to common problems which persist unchallenged, even though there exist feasible and even somewhat advantageous alternatives. Human behavior is, after all, conservative. The necktie appears to be a remarkably functionless, yet persistent, piece of clothing, and the officer's dress saber is clearly an anachronism. The possibility of equally good alternatives to the traditional division of labor and responsibility between sexes in marriage is obvious; and just as obviously, our choices of what to eat are more nearly governed by convention and customs than by nutrition.

One might term these customs and practices which have no clear, contemporary relationship to higher values or to necessities, "autonomous" practices. They are practices which persist on the basis of the general conservatism of human behavior, or on the basis of some secondarily acquired and relatively inconsequential value rather than by virtue of having important purposes, or integral relationships to important aspects of culture. Such autonomous practices, whether they are components of the concept of marriage itself, or whether they are more general, can again become sources of difficulty in the intercultural marriage. Logically, one might suppose that the conflicts generated by differences over such autonomous practices might be readily solved. After all, the practices themselves have, by definition, no vastly important purposes. Nevertheless, they may serve as irritants; as the focal point for conflicts which have private, noncultural elements that are perhaps of greater significance; or simply as component parts of larger difficulties. Precisely because they are, in themselves, relatively unimportant, they become prime vehicles for displacement and substitution when more substantial issues are present. They may then operate to worsen conflict by obscuring its real base and making it less obviously soluble.

Prejudices and Stereotypes

An important source of potential difficulty in the intercultural marriage is that each partner may view the other not as an individual but as the representative of his or her culture or ethnic group. The stereotype to which the marital partner is then expected to conform may seem attractive because it offers a solution to individual psychological problems. Thus, the stereotypic idea that Oriental women are submissive, supportive of their husbands, and serene may appeal strongly to an Occidental man who is fearful of domination and feels he cannot compete effectively for control of a relationship.

Prejudices like these assign to the partner in marriage a specialized role and function which the partner may be quite unwilling to discharge. Since they are usually unspoken, these attitudes constitute a hidden term to the marriage contract which may surface to create difficulties later on. Stereotypes and prejudices may exist in vestigial form, or may not be consciously recognized. Nonetheless, they may operate sufficiently to alter feelings and behavior.

In the example given above, the stereotype is positive, from the point of view of the partner who holds it. A negatively regarded stereotype would obviously be no better, but the major, damaging effect of either would be qualitatively the same: a distortion of the role and personality of the other partner.

The Surrounding Family

Thus far, the discussion has concerned the effects of cultural difference on the marital partners themselves. But many of the difficulties in intercultural marriage may be mediated through the agency of other members of the family: parents, grandparents, siblings, uncles, aunts, cousins, and so on. In most marriages, the persons with the greatest stake in the success of the union and the persons bound by the closest affection ties, are the marital partners themselves. They may therefore strive very hard to be understanding and to handle conflicts carefully. The interest of other relatives in the success of the marriage may be considerably less, and cultural differences may bulk correspondingly larger in their view. They may tend to emphasize the cultural differences which the marital partners try to reduce and compromise. The folklore and mythology of most cultures abound in illustrations at this point.

A Japanese man, for example, is expected to place the needs and desires of his parents and older relatives above those of his wife and children. However, the wife and children clearly have priority in American culture. The Japanese husband of an American wife is clearly in a position of potential conflict. The position his family takes, respecting their culturally sanctioned "rights," may well determine the severity and outcome of this conflict.

In most marriages the original marital unit is augmented by the arrival of children. At this point, difficulties generated by cultural differences may arise. Again, the difficulties may arise not only between the marital partners but between sets of collateral relatives, or between a set of collateral relatives and one of the marital partners. In cultures which place a high value upon the child, or which make having children an especially important goal of marriage, this may be particularly true. In such cultures, questions concerning the education of children, and the arrangements for their physical welfare may be highly sensitive as areas of potential conflict. Finally, the children themselves may introduce elements of conflict between the marital partners by being influenced by one or another set of collateral relatives; or the deleterious effects of culture-conflict upon the children themselves may be sufficient to undermine healthy adjustment, and this in turn may lead to marital difficulties.

An addendum to this discussion of the role of the surrounding family is in order. Not only the surrounding family, but the surrounding society in general, may seriously affect the intercultural marriage. If the society does not accept a particular intercultural marriage, it may place all sorts of barriers in its way: in terms of employment, housing, and even the legal status of the marriage.

The Natural History of Intercultural Marriage

It is not the purpose of this chapter to examine the question of counseling or other treatment for the problems that arise in intercultural marriage. Nonetheless, it may be worthwhile in the context of this brief review of problem areas to outline some of the solutions and outcomes which present themselves for observation. To begin with some rough definitions, a "solution" to the problem of intercultural marriage presumably results in a marriage which endures and which appears to produce sufficient satisfaction for each partner so that neither is obviously and seriously unhappy as the result of it. Obviously, this does not define a "perfect" marriage—if indeed such a phenomenon may be considered to exist. In general, one might say that the successful intercultural marriage should achieve substantially the same degree of happiness, harmony and integrity as does the marriage within a given culture. To go further than this is to invite considerable trouble, since the tests of success tend themselves to be culture bound.

A pattern of solution to the problems raised by intercultural marriage which is not infrequently observed is one that may be termed the "asymmetric solution." One of the marital partners adopts, almost entirely or in large part, the culture of the other, and appears largely to give up his or her own culture. Frequently, although not always, the married couple then live in close proximity with the collateral relatives belonging to the partner whose culture appears to dominate the relationship; or at least, more important relationships are formed with these collateral relatives than with those of the subordinate partner. Again, frequently, although not necessarily, the pattern of the asymmetric solution is consonant both with the prescribed patterns of dominance-within-marriage of the culture which is adopted, and with the private pattern of dominance-submission of the particular couple. For example, a woman of Hawaiian parentage and cultural identity married a Japanese man, and moved into his family's home. She became very much the Japanese wife and mother. Their marriage was patterned in typically Japanese, male-dominant fashion, both as regards public behavior and domestic arrangements and—considerably, although not exclusively—as regards the more private and personal aspects of the marriage.

The asymmetric solution is obviously no guarantee that the marriage will be free of conflict. Certainly, not all intercultural marriages which develop in this way succeed. Nevertheless, it appears to be one of the relatively more stable solutions to the problems presented by intercultural marriage. The alternative "symmetrical" solution, in which each partner gives up some elements of his own culture and adopts some elements of the other's culture, with a rough sort of equivalence, is perhaps less commonly seen. It is more likely to lead to a successful solution when the partners are both rather cosmopolitan, or when the two cultures are relatively similar to one another. It is also more likely to succeed when the married couple is about equally separated from both sets of collateral relatives.

The symmetric solution is far from a simple sharing, or arithmetic division and redistribution of cultural elements. Actually, it would appear in most cases to depend upon a dialectic process, in which the two cultures interact to produce a new cultural synthesis. Some of the elements of the cultural synthesis will presumably be novel as will the arrangement and organization of cultural elements. A classic example of this is to be seen in the culture of Pitcairn Island. Here, the surviving mutineers of H.M.S. *Bounty* and their Tahitian wives founded a culture which, when later studied, was found to contain not only a mixture of elements derived from British and Tahitian cultures, but a distinct group of elements which were unique and duplicated in neither parental culture. Shapiro has documented this point in his *Heritage of the Bounty.* This culture evolved on Pitcairn Island over a period of several generations; but the same thing may be observed on a smaller scale and in nascent state in the individual intercultural marriage.

The symmetric solution tends to appeal to many as being somehow better or worthier than the asymmetric. This is particularly true for individuals whose own cultural background is European or North American. Such persons tend to respond strongly to the democratic and egalitarian qualities of the solution. But this attitude is culture bound, and a culture-bound approach to intercultural marriage is obviously likely to prove dangerous.

In effect, this statement—that culture-bound attitudes are likely to prove dangerous to intercultural marriage—summarizes much of what this chapter has been about. To avoid culture-bound error requires that one be aware of the possibilities for it, and seek pragmatic compromises and solutions for the difficulties it may produce. All the personal qualities and attitudes that militate toward success in any marriage, such as tolerance for diversity, a positive orientation toward change, and flexibility, may be tested to their utmost in the intercultural marriage.

REFERENCES

Bateson, G. Redundancy and coduig. In *Steps to an Ecology of Mind.* New York: Chanceller Publishing Co., 1972.

Birdwhistell, R. *Kinesics and Context.* New York: Chanceller Publishing Co., 1972.

Calkins, F. *My Samoan Chief.* New York: Doubleday and Co., 1962.

Shapiro. H. L. *The Heritage of the Bounty* New York: Simon and Schuster, 1936.

7
Intercultural Marriage and Child Rearing

Eberhard Mann, M.D. and Jane A. Waldron, D.S.W.

This chapter will focus on two major areas: (1) cultural dimensions of child rearing; and (2) the tasks facing the parent and the child in an intercultural marriage. Hawaii's special situation with regard to the number of intercultural marriages, problems in counseling intercultural families, and areas for future research will also be discussed.

Culture and Child Rearing

Child rearing is a task which faces all adults responsible for a child, regardless of cultural identity. Common denominators of this task are set by the developmental phases of the newborn and the growing child, but specific ways of handling the child range widely on the basis of cultural norms and individual variations. A literature survey of child-rearing practices as reported by anthropologists and other observers, gave John Whiting and Irvin Child a wealth of data for a comparative analysis. In their book on *Child Training and Personality,* they document the enormous range of possibilities in handling a child within the same stage of development. For example, regarding the age for weaning, they give the highest culturally reported age as five years, seven months for Chenchu, the lowest as five months for Marquesans, while the median age is about two-and-a-half years. As for toilet training, the highest age for a cultural norm is recorded as four year eight months for Balinese, the lowest as four months for Tanala, while the median falls between the ages of two and three. This data indicates that there are a large number of societies which fall outside the age ranges which may most closely reflect developmental needs and readiness of the child.

Based on the detailed and systematic field work of six cultures, Beatrice and John Whiting illustrated how social behavior of children is the product of several influencing factors in addition to child-rearing practice. Two overall factors, the household structure and the complexity of the socioeconomic system, are identified for such influence. Children brought up in nuclear households were more sociable and intimate in their behavior if compared to those from extended households where authoritative-agressive behavior was more apparent. Children in the simpler cultures, as defined by absence of occupational differentiation, super ordinate authority, and multiple social roles and hierarchies, were more nurturant and responsible if compared with children from the more complex environments whose behavior was more dependent and dominant. On the basis of this study of six cultures, it can be stated that cultural differences in child rearing as antecedents to social behavior of children are of some significance but not exclusively so.

More recently, several investigators have taken a closer look at the specific cultural differences of child rearing between two societies, the American cultural majority usually serving as a reference point. Barry Brazelton, a pediatrician, during his visit to a Mayan village in Mexico, found that the handling of the infants there varies considerably from that of middle-class Americans. After birth and throughout the first year, the baby is clad with a long heavy skirt extending beyond the feet. This skirt is held in place by a wide belt cinch, wrapped firmly around the abdomen. The swaddling acts as a constant suppressant of motor activity and prevents exploratory activities. Except for feeding, the infant's face is also covered, especially during the first three months; such a practice reduces visual stimulation to a minimum.

Striking is the frequent nursing of the infant. Breast feeding is performed in response to activity of the infant rather than to a more direct expression of hunger. A baby is never allowed to cry—from hunger or from becoming too active. In general, social, verbal, and visual stimulation are minimal during the first year, while kinesthetic and tactile forms of interaction are maximal.

Mothers in this culture thus set up a mode of immediate contingent responsiveness to the infant's needs—before he can build up to express a need and feel the importance of it, make a demand and then find it gratified. There is little experience in early infancy which could contribute to the framework for self-motivated demand, frustration and then gratification—a cycle which must be important in fueling a model for self-initiated and reinforced independence.

William Caudill, an anthropologist, compared in carefully monitored detail the child-rearing patterns of mothers in Japan and those of mothers in America. An American mother, according to Caudill, sees her baby from birth as a separate and autonomous individual with his own needs and desires. Therefore, she helps him to express these needs and desires through her emphasis on vocal communication. Separateness and independence are stressed by having the infant sleep in his own crib shortly after birth; early weaning from breast or bottle and teaching self-feeding skills usually before the end of the first year are the rule. Exploration of the body or environment is welcomed. The baby is lightly dressed or frequently naked; movement is encouraged. Toilet training becomes an important issue in teaching children to take care of their own bodily functions at an early age. Psychologically, American child rearing appears to be directed towards sharpening ego boundaries.

In contrast, the Japanese mother appears to view her child more as an extension of herself. Ego boundaries in the Japanese are more blurred. There is less need for the infant to tell his mother verbally what he wants because, after all, they are virtually one. More emphasis is placed on physical communication. The Japanese mother rocks, lulls, soothes, and sleeps with her infant and thus gratifies and indulges dependent needs, while autonomous strivings are less fostered.

Impressionistic reports of child-rearing patterns in other cultures reveal similar evidence that links variations in the way infants and young children are cared for to differences in adult behaviors that are then seen as part of the cultural character for that group of people.

According to Wen-Shing Tseng and Jing Hsu, in the Chinese culture infants are breastfed on demand, nursing is prolonged and weaning unhurried. Babies are carried on the mother's back during the day and sleep in the parent's bed at night. Toilet training is permissive, with the mother training herself to recognize the child's needs and to take care of them. Whereas gratification and dependency are stressed, the expression of aggression is discouraged. Open and active expression of anger is strongly discouraged, competition shamed, and self-accomplishment belittled. These child-rearing practices appear closely linked to the general cultural characteristics of emphasis on the extended family, fixed familial and sex roles, and delayed development of independence for even young adults.

Gregory Bateson and Margaret Mead in their detailed reports on Balinese child rearing pointed out rigid constraints that exist regarding the expression of autonomy. The infant is carried in a sling with his right hand bound to his side, forcing passive accommodation. Speech is taught by imitation of phrases. These constraints which appear to lead to passive experiencing of the world have been felt to play a part in the ability of the Balinese to enter readily into trance states so much a part of ceremonial dance performances.

Adeoye Lumbo, an African psychiatrist, has suggested that the flexibility and security found in many of the peoples in various African cultures can be traced to early child rearing techniques which emphasize gratifying the infant, and to the role of the extended family in the care of the child. Custom prescribes breast feeding for an almost indefinite period. The mother carries the infant on her back, occasionally putting him down to sleep, but more often he sleeps on his mother's, grandmother's or older sister's back. From time to time he is held by some other member of the family. The child thus easily becomes accustomed to these sorties into strange arms with varying degrees of contact, comfort, and security. At the age of three when the child is transferred to the grandparents or older siblings, he does not feel rejected, since he has learned to accept substitutes early.

Most of the reports presented, above all, indicate that there is considerable variation of child-rearing practice among different cultural backgrounds. More importantly, beyond the practice of child rearing are basic ideas and philosophies such as the emphasis on independence and individuality, the value of conformity and obligation. Associated with urbanization and industrialization, traditional processes have often been disrupted, altered, and modified. This, coupled with the greater frequency of intercultural marriage, has made it increasingly difficult to predict exactly what will happen when partners of different cultures set about to raise children. It is clear, however, from the consideration of different cultural styles and purposes played out in child-rearing patterns, that different child-rearing patterns may have contradictory aims, and therefore present the couple involved with considerable challenge and stress when those methods and aims conflict.

Child Rearing in Intercultural Families

Intercultural marriage refers to a marriage occurring between partners of different cultural backgrounds. Being a spouse in an intercultural marriage is different from being a parent in such a marriage. Even when the couple has seemingly worked through cultural differences the advent of the first child is likely to bring a resurgence of old conflicts over culture. Anticipating parenthood sets the stage for regression into one's own powerful childhood experiences and may give rise to emotions which surprise and can overwhelm both partners. As Paul L. Adams points out, old prejudices and identifications have to be reworked. The mother-to-be must come to some tenable truce with her own mother in order to prepare to be a mother. Although the same themes of growth, dependence and identification characterize the culturally mixed as well as the culturally homogenous family, cultural differences add another dimension.

For example, a mother-to-be who has discussed the issue of a mixed ethnic child with her husband openly and thinks herself free of ethnic and racial concerns may suddenly become extremely worried about the child's looks, the color of his skin, his facial features. A Caucasian mother may ask herself whether she wants to give birth to a child who is not like her, but "yellow and slant-eyed" like her Oriental husband. Does she "have the right to put such a child into this world?" The Oriental father may be concerned about how his parents and relatives will react to the racially mixed baby. If the extended family subtly or openly objected to the marriage, a "different looking child" might increase feelings of rejection in the parent and alienate him further from his group, resulting in resentment of the spouse or the child. If this conflict stays unresolved, the child will experience from the start an ambivalent acceptance which will have damaging effects on his own development of trust and self-esteem.

Each developmental stage, whether it involves issues of dependency, autonomy, power, skill mastery, sex identification, values, educational experiences, or peer relations, will more easily create conflicts when the culturally different parents adhere to variant prescriptions of how to achieve desired behaviors. A Caucasian husband may feel neglected by his Japanese wife when after childbirth she turns her attention quite exclusively to the baby corresponding to her culturally determined perception of her maternal role. Arguments may arise about mother "pampering" and "spoiling" the children by gratifying their dependency needs rather than fostering independent strivings. A Chinese father might feel sabotaged in his attempt to raise obedient, achieving children when the Caucasian mother "behind his back" allows more freedom for her youngsters and does not get upset over occasional fights or behavior complaints from the teachers since she values these behaviors as indications of assertiveness. For father these same behaviors might represent a violation of respect towards the elders and might be seen as shameful. While in Caucasian families children tend to be treated more as individuals in their own right, in traditional Chinese families roles for children according to birth, rank, and sex are most clearly defined. The special importance of the first born son as an extension, inheritor, and later as caretaker of the family might become a conflictual issue in an intermarried family, when the Caucasian partner supports and fosters attempts of the son to break away from family ties, seeing the attempts as "natural," and accusing the Chinese partner of "unfairness," "harshness," and "rigidity."

Thus, in an intercultural marriage, every developmental stage may turn into a potentially stressful situation between the parents themselves or between the parent and the child. Which stage in the development becomes problematic will depend on the relationship of many factors, including the cultural mix, the strength of either parent's adherence to tradition, their personality structure, or the families' integration into the broader social environment.

Problems of identification present a major stress on the child from an intercultural—and more so from an interracial—family. Skin color alone is loaded heavily with social implications. According to Erick Erikson, unresolved racial conflicts will affect the parents' ability to care for the infant in a nurturant way and leave the child with a deep sense of not belonging and insecurity. Awareness of physical difference occurs early. By age three the child can distinguish color differences within his family. By ages four to five years the child is able to talk about skin color. At this time the first signs of racial discrimination emerge. Both white and black children, in a study by Harold Stevenson and others, prefer the physical characteristics of white children and assigned more negative attributes to black children. Unfortunately, no such studies exist for other racial minorities like Orientals or Spanish-speaking groups. Questions of identity formation in mixed children are also largely unresearched. Does girl child identify with her mother and a boy with his father regardless of appearance? Are there shifts at certain developmental stages? How much does physical similarity influence identification regardless of sex?

Erikson contends that children identify initially with the aspects of people by which they themselves are most immediately affected, their identification with parents centering in certain over-valued and ill-understood body parts, capacities, and role appearance. Later comes the importance of society's identifying the young individual, recognizing and accepting him as he is. From preschool on, the racially mixed child is confronted with society's perception of him which does not in many cases coincide with his own image that has been drawn from his parents. For example, a child of a black-white family will be seen in our society mostly as black yet may be rejected by an increasingly proud black society. A mixed child who has identified for various reasons with one parent may find out later that this does not fit social reality. Once a child learns that one part of him belongs to a "superordinate" group, he might be unwilling to identify with the "subordinate" part but he will also find out that he is not easily accepted as equal into the more highly esteemed group.

In the late twenties, Stonequist created the term "the marginal man" as a characterization of the mulatto who often finds himself cut off from both cultures he originated from. This loss of cultural identity resulted in excessive self-consciousness, ambivalence in attitude and sentiment, inferiority complexes or compensatory superiority complexes, hypersensitiveness with a tendency to rationalize aggressiveness, and a tendency to be critical in a manner which is more imitative and conformist rather than creative in most instances. Certainly the civil rights movement has begun to change attitudes about the acceptance of the black or part-black man, but the same problems confront any offspring of mixed racial background where the environment operates with prejudice.

A Case Example

The following illustrates a situation in which cultural differences turned into a disaster. It has to be pointed out that the course this particular family took is extreme and much determined by the parents' immature personalities; most families, no doubt, are likely to find healthier solutions. However, this case seems to clearly highlight many of the conflictual areas which can face intercultural families.

Martha O., an eleven-year-old daughter of a European teacher and a Japanese college-educated housewife was admitted to a children's residential treatment center for grossly psychotic symptoms. She exhibited auditory and visual hallucinations, seeing and hearing "dead people all around." She was in a continuous state of panic, screamed uncontrollably, and was preoccupied with delusional thoughts of death and destruction—"There is this lightning which should hit my house—it should kill them inside; when I lose I gain." She was confused calling various staff members or children "mother, father or brothers," clinging or swearing at them interchangeably in English and Japanese.

The information obtained from both parents allowed us to follow the development of this family from the beginning of their union. Their life seemed to be characterized by a sequence of crises, each of which influenced the next step in their development. Mr. O. met his wife in Japan, where he had been living for two years teaching English at a small private language institute. He had left Scotland "because that country was impossible to live in—not providing job opportunities." He also resented the "materialistic mind" of his fellow countrymen. He married his wife due to "an accident"—by which he meant her first pregnancy—considering Oriental women as "homely servants," but not as "adequate partners for life." Mrs. O. saw in the acquaintance with Mr. O. a possibility to "escape my old-fashioned family" and she believed that "Western men respected their women more for what they are and want than Japanese men."

68

Already now the first difficulties become evident. This couple based their relationship on culturally stereotyped images to a degree which prevented exploration of each other's idiosyncratic personalities. Mr. O., who was a professional and social failure in his homeland, had immigrated to a country whose culture he saw as "second rate." This permitted him gratification of his unfulfilled needs of dominance, and he projected his sense of inferiority to the Oriental race. In his mind, a marriage with a Japanese represented a move downward on the social scale.

For Mrs. O., who was in conflict with modern and traditional Japanese values, a union with a Westerner meant "liberation, personal respect and higher social esteem." Since their mutual conflicting prejudices and expectations clouded their ability to assess the reality of the situation, their marriage began badly.

Once pregnant and married, Mrs. O. had to realize that this dream of "liberation" was an illusion she was not able to cope with. Since her husband rejected her requests for guidance and protection, she tried to return to her parents for help. Economically affluent, her parents provided her with money and a maid, but made clear that she had brought "shame on the family by marrying a foreigner; that she was a loose woman and not welcomed home with a foreign child." At this point she began to contemplate abortion or suicide. Mr. O. interpreted his wife's employment of a maid as an "abdication from her responsibilities as a mother and as laziness."

We must consider that attitudes of racial purity common among Japanese have also been inculcated in Mrs. O., and that only pressures of her personal situation enabled her to act contrary to general Japanese preferences in marrying outside her race. The concern of Japanese with racial purity is amply documented, and we may assume that both at home and outside Martha encountered subtle and not so subtle signs of disapproval of the marriage and the child as a product of this union. The complexity of culturally objectionable practices and guilt over the effects of her behavior on her own family in Mrs. O.'s case must have caused her to live in continuous inner turmoil which, in turn, was fanned by the lack of cultural sensitivity to her feelings and emotions on the part of the Occidental husband. Cultural ideas about race, therefore, engendered severe pressures on the marital relationship of Martha's parents, while identity questions of the racially mixed child in the context of these conflicting beliefs characterized Martha's situation, as we will see.

Martha made her entrance into the world in an atmosphere of resentment, fear, and anger. Father felt more "stuck," since his wife refused a divorce to avoid another "scandal"; she did not know where to turn along with an "alien child" which would make her look like a "prostitute." Child care during Martha's first year of life was left predominantly to the maid, who, in father's words was "stubborn and influenced by mother" and according to mother was "confused by father's harshness." Father objected mainly to the child's being constantly carried and sleeping with the maid. He felt that a child from early age had to learn to "get around without the help of others." In his view "weaklings" resulted from giving them "everything they cried for." He insisted on feeding according to schedule rather than demand, having her sleep alone in a crib and letting her cry, attitudes which mother felt to be "very cruel." Out of fear of being beaten by her husband, she did not interfere, however, but began to view her now one-year-old daughter "as a monster" who "screamed so much that I could never calm her while father enjoyed his daughter becoming so talkative." When Martha began crawling father spent more time with her teaching her to use spoons, teaching her to walk and move about, which according to mother made Martha "a wild, disobedient" child. The maid left after one year stating she could not do her work with a "crazy man."

The difference in child rearing practices and values between Japanese and Western culture are reflected in this case. Since in our case example both parents continued to reject each other's child rearing approaches and undermined each other's role as an efficient parent, problems in the child's development could be predicted. Instead of being entrusted with loving acceptance, from birth Martha experienced and incorporated the parent's ambivalence with unresolved questions about who she was, to whom she belonged, and who she could trust, themes which returned dramatically during her psychotic break, when infantile panic states, rages, destructiveness, and fear of abandonment surfaced.

During the next several years Mr. and Mrs. O. began to live in a more parallel fashion. Communication between them was marginal, but it reduced the frequency of violent clashes. Mrs. O. found work in a restaurant, which allowed her a new small circle of Japanese friends. She stated that she felt distant from Martha, who did not look Japanese at all but more "Italian" with "big brown eyes and brown hair." She was afraid of her daughter's temper tantrums and left child care entirely to her husband. When Martha entered a Japanese kindergarten at age four, the teachers complained that she assaulted her peers and seemed a "very angry girl." Father felt the teachers did not like her because she looked like a Caucasian, and he described Martha as becoming "unhappy," "clinging to me and crying all the time, never wanting to leave the house" during this period. He finally kept her at home and enrolled her only again at the age of six years in an international school, where Martha apparently did better, although she had difficulties making friends.

Peers become increasingly important as children reach school age.

This coincides at a time when, according to Adams, "agemates are ossifying in all of their racial stereotypes." On the surface Martha identified herself more as a Caucasian, aided by her looks and alienation from mother. Her peers also perceived her in this role. With a basic poor self-image this led to negative perceptions of her Japanese peer group, anxiety, and behavior problems. In a more mixed environment she felt safer but was unable to enter age-appropriate relationships. Piskacek points out that

"an organism cannot tolerate a permanent state of tension. If there is no resolution and integration, there is maladjustment. . . . An interracial child is left to his own desires. He is truly representative of class of one. He cannot be supported by the defenses that the culture provides. He cannot profit from the experience of his parents and share their defenses since they are a product of a different, homogeneous background and will never be able to experience his position. . . . What compensatory mechanism are then available to the child? He may choose to overidentify with one race [in Martha's case, as a Caucasian] as a defense against identity confusion, which might paradoxically lead to an actual loss of identity [no feeling of belonging]. Another solution is negative identification with rejection of one part of identity [Martha's Japanese heritage]. . . . There is also a standstill solution leading to alienation and depersonalization, resulting in final distortion of personality [dramatically evidenced in Martha's final psychotic disorganization].

The parents' arrangement to live parallel lives seemed at least to help Mrs. O. regain some self-confidence. Four years after Martha's birth she decided to have "another child for myself" and gave birth to a son. This time she managed to take care of the baby herself, actively opposing father's interference. Feeling assured by "affectionate" responses from the boy, she gave birth to another boy two years later and took care of him as well, experiencing for the first time satisfaction "to be a mother." The boys happened to look more Oriental than Caucasian and integrated better in their Japanese environment and peer group. Although they were not free of symptoms—mainly multiple somatic problems like vomiting, asthma, or headaches which cleared outside the house—they were more "manageable" and "happy." For Martha the arrival of her two brothers, however, precipitated a new crisis. She "abused" and "tortured" her older baby brother and undertook a suicide attempt (ingestion of tranquilizers) when the second boy was born. Later she demanded a Caucasian brother, a Caucasian mother, accused her brothers of not loving her and fought constantly with them.

Sibling rivalry among interracial families adds another dimension if marital equilibrium fosters the development of subgroups within the family and competition for the child's loyalty prevails. Shades of color and

71

physiognomy contribute to the uncertainty about themselves and their roles.

Finally, three years ago, Mrs. O. decided to work towards a divorce and remarry a Japanese man in order to have "a family like everybody else." Afraid of causing another scandal, however, and seeing difficulties in finding a Japanese partner in Japan with three mixed children, she convinced her husband to immigrate to Hawaii. There she hoped to find a more accepting environment, especially for Martha, since "many races live in Hawaii peacefully together." Economically the move to Hawaii was a disaster. Father did not find work, since his teaching credentials were insufficient and his visa status unclear. The couple's relationship deteriorated rapidly with much violence reemerging.

Finally, after eighteen months Mrs. O. obtained a divorce. She remarried within one week a traditional second-generation Japanese-American business man, who was willing to adopt all three children. The court awarded custody to mother for reasons of economic stability, but granted father liberal visiting rights. While the boys voiced contentment about the "quiet new home with Mom not fighting with Bill [their stepfather] all the time as she did with Dad," Martha resented the "Japanese slit eye, who wants to be my father, but never will." She frequently ran away from mother's house to her father and became increasingly withdrawn, until she developed the symptoms which led to her hospitalization.

With mother's remarriage the boys seemed to find relief from the anxiety over the parents' unsettled emotions. It stabilized their identification as "more Japanese." For Martha the remarriage constituted an intolerable stress. A "new Japanese father" increased the stigma of being different and she felt like an outcase in her new home. After the subsidence of her acute symptoms, Martha began to express her feelings of despair, seeing herself as the cause of her parents' separation. "I am someone who does not belong anywhere and is not wanted anywhere and makes everybody unhappy."

Our participation in this family's life history ended as abruptly as it began: Mr. O. left the United States with all three children for an unknown destination without notifying his former wife. New crises can be predicted for Martha, who enters adolescence in a state of confused identity, unable to integrate her double cultural heritage.

Hawaii's Mixed Children

In contrast to the mainland United States, Hawaii is an interethnic melting pot. No racial group forms a distinct majority. Figures from Hawaii State Health Surveillance, 1973, indicates that the larger groups are

Caucasians (29.1 percent), Japanese (26.8 percent), Hawaiians, part-Hawaiians (19.2 percent), Filipinos (7.8 percent), "Unknown-Mixed" (9.8 percent), Chinese (4.4 percent). Blacks, Koreans, Samoans, Puerto Ricans, and others form smaller groups, with only Samoans constituting more than 1 percent of the total population. Within the Caucasians, the Portuguese form a fairly distinct group. Blacks are mostly transients in the military. Since it is against the law for public agencies to inquire about ethnic background, estimates are frequently derived from names and looks only. Therefore, no reliable data exist to denote specific ethnic backgrounds in the mixed or part-Hawaiian category. This hampers interethnic research considerably.

Intermarriages in Hawaii are as frequent as unicultural marriages. Mixed racial children, therefore, are not rarity, and the use of the term "cosmopolitan" is common to describe a mixed cultural background such as "Chinese-Hawaiian-Filipino-Irish."

In February 1975 the authors met with a group of high school students to discuss "growing up with parents from different cultures." Except for one "sansei" girl, third generation Japanese in Hawaii, all adolescents were of mixed blood, predominantly of Hawaiian-Asian or Hawaiian-Caucasian background. The ages of the participants ranged from fourteen to sixteen years. Most of the parents of these adolescents had been born and raised in Hawaii. The students were eager to participate, and there was easy communication between them and the two Caucasian interviewers. Several observations seemed remarkable. The topic of ethnic differences never came up spontaneously. Instead, issues the group seemed pressured to discuss were more clearly adolescent issues: difficult times with old-fashioned parents, complaints about house chores, school hassles, boy and girlfriend topics, and so forth. When the group was urged to focus on their feelings and ideas about their ethnic backgrounds, in almost every case the influence of dual culture was denied. Referring to behavioral characteristics of their parents, they used cultural stereotypes; that is Hawaiians were "easygoing, soft hearted, sharing, people loving;" Chinese were "strict and quiet;" Japanese had "exact rules; girls had to stay in the house and boys were encouraged to find a career;" Caucasians were "big mouth" and Filipinos were "moody and taking everything in." When going into specifics about their parents' attitudes, however, it became clear that the generalizations did not fit that well. There were strict Hawaiian fathers, soft-hearted, outgoing Chinese mothers and quiet Caucasian parents. The students felt that the cultural background of their ideal future partner was irrelevant as long as they were "considerate." The majority, however, admitted that their parents had at one time or another mentioned that they did not want their children to marry a black.

Although the feelings of the adolescents in this group cannot be taken to be representative of all children from mixed ethnic backgrounds, for them—at a conscious level—their mixed cultural heritage did not constitute a major conflict area. Difficulties between children and parents, as they saw it, depended largely on differences between traditional and modern ways of acting and thinking and they described the usual conflicts between generations.

Once they were coerced into giving cultural issues some consideration, they initially responded with the common stereotypic ethnic descriptions, even though these were clearly contradicted by their actual life experiences. This could indicate some insecurity and confusion about their own identification. There was a tendency to identify themselves as "just local," when a clear-cut cultural heritage did not exist. By being a "local" they seemed to gain needed membership in a group distinct from other defined ethnic populations.

In a separate talk with the school counselor' a part-Hawaiian, it was learned that the majority of these adolescents was seen by their mostly Oriental teachers as having behavior problems such as drug abuse, absenteeism, classroom disruption, and poor grades, and that many had at one time or another been in conflict with the law.

This counselor lead a "human relations" club, which was less focused on academic tasks; emphasis was placed more on joint discussions, planning and completing social tasks including organizing school camps, filmmaking or publicizing articles about various topics of interest in their school or local newspapers. This class, which relied on cooperation and teamwork without grading individual performance was very popular among mixed youths, while others like Caucasians, Japanese, Chinese or Koreans were only sparsely represented in spite of many invitations.

Recent statistics published by the Hawaiian Association of Asian and Pacific People (HAAPP) showed that mixed families, including part-Hawaiians, are overpresented among the "disadvantaged" population in many aspects. Part-Hawaiians and other mixes represent roughly 14 percent of the total state population. However, juveniles in this group have a share of more than 50 percent among the residents of the State Youth Correctional Facility. Equally, the percentage of part-Hawaiians served by a private rehabilitation agency, the Howard Johnson Association, is nearly four times higher than the state's total part-Hawaiian population. Part-Hawaiians and other mixes are found in disproportionately low numbers in high achievement schools, swell the ranks of school dropouts, absentees, and suspendees. Their families are overpresented among those on public welfare assistance.

Invariably, the providers of these various services belong to ethnic groups who are mostly underrepresented as consumers. For example, the percentage of Japanese probation officers totals more than half the entire family court probation staff, while the number of Japanese residents in the Youth Correctional Facility represent the lowest for any ethnic group in relation to their population in the state. Similar discrepancies exist in the ethnic composition of school teachers or public agency workers. Mental health clinics are less frequently visited by part-Hawaiians than by other ethnic groups. These studies indicate a high degree of isolation and alienation of a large part of the mixed population group from the dominant social system, which promotes Western, middle-class, and achievement oriented values. Hawaiian Association of Asian and Pacific People points out that cultural factors associated with behavior problems are unfortunately rarely focused on by the services mentioned. For example, school drop-out or suspension evaluations usually do not go beyond the immediate school environment when they express "dislike of school activities, behavioral difficulties, such as smoking, truancy, fighting, failure to conform to school requirements and academic difficulty." Cultural, social, and psychological factors are not explained. A large number of children with school problems are not adequately reached by counseling services, and no data is available to relate ethnicity to counseling response.

These data underline an urgent need for expanded interethnic research in order to develop special education programs which allow consideration of the sociocultural particularities of various ethnic groups. The "mixed" group seems to be the most disadvantaged with a lack of helping resources and agencies by whom they feel understood.

Treatment of Intercultural Parents and Their Children

Literature on the treatment of intercultural families is very sparse and remains a big area for research. The problems seem much clearer, however, than the solutions. Some of the difficulties in the treatment of parents and children of intercultural marriages can be seen in the followng case description.

Elsa M., a seven-year-old daughter of a Hong Kong-born Chinese father and an American Caucasian mother, was admitted to a children's mental health inpatient unit. Elsa had exhibited bizarre behavior since age three after a near drowning accident and was described as being uncontrollable since six months. The problem behaviors involved incessant pulling and twirling hair, baby talk, open masturbation and exposure of genitals at school, and severe temper tantrums. Elsa was the second of four children. Her ten-year-old brother reportedly showed some minor behavior disturbances at school, that is, whining, tattling, and signs of hyperactivity, while two younger sisters were allegedly doing well. Both parents were college educated; father taught at an elementary school and mother was a housewife. The parents disagreed continuously with each other about child rearing matters and held each other responsible for Elsa's problem. Father accused mother of being sloppy, lazy, and too punitive, showing little concern or love for her daughter; while mother renounced bitterly father's different standards in disciplining the children. She complained that her husband was overly rigid and strict with his son and too permissive with his "sick" daughter. Both parents felt that cultural differences did not account for their problems since they had discussed them out in the past.

The therapeutic team consisted of a German-born child psychiatrist, a Hawaii-born social worker of Korean background, and a Hong Kong-born and raised Chinese social worker student. Within the team much of the discussion initially focused on whether cultural differences led to the clashes between the parents which victimized the child-patient. Cultural etiology was especially emphasized by the Caucasian psychiatrist in regards to the Chinese husband. It seemed fairly obvious to him that Mr. M. was struggling with his culturally determined role as husband and father. When Mr. M. stated that he was "tired of having to discuss everything twice before something got done," the clinician saw this as a culture-syntonic demand for unquestioned obedience and authority. When Mr. M. reprimanded his son harshly for not sitting straight on a chair but allowed his daughter to run around in the room, the psychiatrist explained this in terms of the father's role expectations: in China the oldest son fulfilled a special function as successive leader of the family, having to present a continuous example of good, respectful conduct, while the girls were still in an age where irresponsible behaviors could be indulged. In contrast, in Mrs. M. the psychiatrist saw less of the conflictual behaviors influenced by her American culture. Her silent but "pervasive, childlike" resistance to all her husband's orders, for example, not keeping the house in order or treating her children in opposition to what her husband demanded or refusing sexual relations out of "anger," were psychologically explained in terms of a hysterical neurosis.

The Chinese social worker student saw in Mrs. M.'s "dislike of household work," "flexibility" and "encouragement" of the children's "free expression," attributes of Western culture. She clearly could not detect many typical Chinese behaviors in Mr. M., whom she found a "very insecure personality," which accounted for his "fear of discussions and compensatory rigidity."

At times, the Korean social worker had to serve as intermediary between the other two team members, posing more pragmatic considerations. Since all three therapists agreed that intermarital conflict had been displaced on the identified child-patient, couple's therapy was considered the treatment of choice. Elsa M. improved rapidly to the level of a normal seven-year-old girl once the parents were not using her as their focus of conflict. Six months after her discharge back home she was doing well. Although her parents continued to have differences, they were more aware of the conflicts between them and were more able to deal with them directly without using their children for their struggles. In therapy, emphasis was on communication techniques, while cultural issues were not stressed since they were considered irrelevant by both parents. A therapist faced with an intercultural family often finds himself uncomfortable if he has not had experience with such situations. Clearly there is much more difficulty in sorting out dynamics and in deriving effective treatment plans when a variety of cultural influences must be considered. How much the therapist's own cultural heritage will distort an objective view of the family's actual situation is a major question. The therapist is apt to unwittingly identify with the spouse of his background or, in fear of this, may unduly support the partner of the different cultural background. An important question is, when does he emphasize cultural aspects or deny them?

At first glance, the detection of cultural differences seems to be fairly easy to the naive observer from another culture, where the complexity apparent in a familiar setting is cut away. In our case example Chinese culture traits in Mr. M. were, in the eyes of the Caucasian psychiatrist, as "obvious" as Western values in Mrs. M. were "clearly" visible to the Chinese social worker. However, when understanding of a new culture increases, the complexity is uncovered and issues lose their simplicity.

The effect of the therapist on a culturally different client must be seen as an important ingredient in therapy. What does he do when he is accused of favoritism or ethnic prejudice by a member of a family who uses such charges to manipulate the other family members or the therapist? When is a child or adolescent using his "mixed blood" as a potent justification for antisocial behavior, since an "unjust society deserves it"; or when is discrimination heavily influencing the development of antisocial, delinquent behavior in a patient? Knowlege of the cultures concerned will naturally increase sensitivity to such a complex situation. Cultural generalizations or simplifications, however, can prove detrimental if they are applied without careful assessment. For example, a withdrawn, clinging first grader is not necessarily so because his mother is a protective, overindulgent Japanese mother. A cotherapist matching the "other" patient's culture also does not necessarily prove an asset to the therapy. The dangers of overidentification can be as problematic as insensitive or prejudicial attitudes. A mixed therapeutic team that functions well, however, may serve as a model that cultural differences do not prevent the development of sound interpersonal relationships. They can demonstrate that their diversity offers rich opportunities to widen one's own limited horizons. They can also show that many disagreements are the result of the usual daily life struggles with intimacy and relationships which are worked out around issues involving money, food, and work, and which are not very different from other families. Cultural differences provide more variation for the ways in which family members express themselves and thus provide more areas for discord. On the positive side, the presence of two or more cultures also provides more richness and variation in solutions to the tasks of everyday living.

In order to diminish resistance, the therapist should be ready to discuss his own feelings about cultural differences early in treatment. That there is no culture-free approach should be acknowledged, and the potential for personal growth which is offered through integration of a dual heritage should be emphasized.

One can assume that for most intercultural families, traditional individual psychoanalysis will not be very effective since it does not take into account external reality forces which may be critical for understanding. Since the cultural determinants of thinking and feeling are largely unconscious and probably also unfamiliar to the therapist, observation of the context in which behavior occurs might prevent misinterpretation based upon cultural ignorance. Family therapy enables the therapist to look at cultural systems and can aid in the therapist's ability to formulate a more accurate assessment of the situation.

Paul Adams points out that parental counseling in culturally mixed families often is concerned with problems pertaining much more to their special backgrounds, and that these families are characterized as much by themes of growth, caring, and identification as unicultural families. The therapist has to recognize when a family has reached a stage where their real difficulty is more likely to be in getting some pleasure from parenthood, and their concern over ethnicity becomes secondary. In regard to counseling adolescents of mixed parentage who, besides the problems of their compeers have "especially poignant twists to the task of finding their identity as adults," Adams states that counselors stand fairly secure when they convey to the teenager that they approve of his interethnic family, even though they may not approve of everything about his parents. They help him best by exploring the "racial thing" but then are willing to say "Okay, now, other than the race thing, you have some problems I might help you with."

If parents are unified in their alliance, there will be less ambivalence about their children's cultural identity and they more probably will be able to negotiate the various developmental stages of their children with some degree of success. From birth the child learns to see himself as he is seen by his parents. If he is accepted and supported, not pulled apart, he is more likely to develop an integrated image of himself. Acceptance by the extended families and the surrounding society will reduce the prejudicial stresses. Fortunately our society seems to be moving toward this direction, albeit slowly and with hesitation.

Areas for Future Study

As states earlier, the area of intercultural child rearing is a blank field on the psychiatric and sociological research map. The literature cited here consists mainly of impressionistic case material from a selected population who asked for psychiatric help. The issues discussed in this chapter raise more questions than they provide answers. To explore some of the problems one would have to begin with a systematic collection of data regarding the relationship of psychopathology to intercultural factors in child rearing. Child-rearing practices at different stages of child development in intercultural families have to be compared with unicultural groups of origin in order to obtain information about their influence on personality development. The dynamics of identity formation in culturally mixed children need to be explored. Socialization patterns in intercultural families need to be examined and correlated to personality development. An understanding of mechanisms of adaptation in healthy mixed racial families are practically nonexistent and need to be researched. Only with more knowledge can the complex relationship between intercultural marriage and child rearing be understood, and it is only with such understanding that more realistic and effective prevention and therapeutic programs can be devised.

REFERENCES

Adams, P. Counseling with interracial couples and their children in the South. In *Interracial Marriage: Expectation and Realities.* Edited by I. Stuart and L. E. Abt. New York: Grossman Publishers, 1973.

Bateson, G. and Mead, M. *The Balinese Character.* Vol. 2, Special publication of the New York Academy of Science, 1942.

Brazelton, T. B. Implications of infant development among the Mayan Indians of Mexico. *Human Development* 15:90-111, 1972.

Caudill, W. and Schooler, C. Child behavior and child rearing in Japan and in the United States. *Journal of Nervous and Mental Disease* 157:323-337, 1973.

Caudill, W. and Weinstein, H. Maternal care and infant behavior in Japan and America. *Psychiatry* 32:12-43, 1969.

Doi, T. *The Anatomy of Dependence.* Tokyo: Kodansha International, 1973.

Erikson, E. H. Identity and the life cycle. *Psychological Issues,* No. 1, 1-171, 1959.

Lambo, A. The vulnerable African child. *The Child in His Family Risk.* E. J. Anthony and C. Kouperiik. New York: John Wiley and Sons, 1974.

Piskacek, V. and Golub, M. Children of interracial marriages. *Interracial Marriages: Expectation and Realities.* Edited by I. Stuart and L. E. Abt. New York: Grossman Publishers, 1973.

Scofield, R. and Sun, C. W. A comparative study of the differential effect upon personality of Chinese and American child training practices. *The Journal of Social Psychology* 52:221-224, 1960.

Silberman, C. E. *Crisis in Black and White.* New York: Random House, 1964.

Stevenson, H. and Stewart, E. A developmental study of racial awareness in young children. *Child Development* 29:399-409, 1958.

Tseng, W. S. and Hsu, J. Chinese culture, personality formation and mental illness. *Internations Journal of Social Psychiatry* 16:5-14, 1969.

Whiting, J. and Child, I. *Child Training and Personality.* New Haven: Yale University Press, 1953.

Whiting, B. B. *Six Cultures: Studies of Child Rearing,* New York: John Wiley, 1963.

Young, B. A shared beginning: An Asian and Pacific perspective of social conditions in Hawaii. *Hawaii Association of Asian and Pacific Peoples.* The proceedings of the HAAPP Statewide Mental Health Conference, June, 1974.

8
Intercultural Family Interaction Patterns

John F. McDermott, Jr., M.D. and Chantis Fukunaga

The family is a crucial organism for the transmission of culture from one generation to another; this particular function of the family works relatively smoothly in ethnically homogeneous marriages, but when the marital partners are of different ancestry, then the complication of two different cultures is introduced and the task becomes an extremely difficult one of harmonizing two different cultures, and smoothly transmitting the result to the descendants.

In the previous chapter, the reader has become acquainted with the breadth and depth of the research done on intercultural marriage with special reference to its effect on the development of children. The research suggests that if parental attitudes and values conflict or are inconsistent, they are likely to lead to difficulties in the children's development, with particular problems of identity formation, that is the sense each individual has of who he is, where he came from, and where he is going.

This chapter will extend this theme from those studies and the reports of special groups of individuals and their families. We will attempt to provide the reader with some actual child psychiatric experience from the John A. Burns School of Medicine, Department of Psychiatry. When families of intercultural marriages seek help for a problem child, we are able to observe first-hand the effect of disharmony of maternal and paternal cultural backgrounds on the children. We recognize, of course, that not all parental behaviors are primarily culturally determined; many are personal and familial. But we have attempted to focus on those that appear to have a strong cultural origin.

It is hoped that from this approach some of the "risks" of intercultural marriage in the rearing of children can thereby be identified and that parents will find it easier to discover solutions, or, even more important, to anticipate and prevent problems which might adversely affect their children's development. Intercultural marriages in the mid-1970s amounted to 50 percent of the marriages in the state of Hawaii. Thus, they are the statistical norm in Hawaii's society, becoming the new "mixed" marriages, replacing those of differing religions from which the term originated. Two adults can make a conscious choice in which each recognizes his or her own family traditions, the relationship of those traditions to those of the spouse, and potential points of conflicts as well as of merging. New combinations forming new lifestyle patterns for these marriages are common. However, much like stepfamilies, in which two partial families unite, these marriages also carry with them their own special history with strong traditions, expectations, and other values, both open and hidden, which continue to influence each partner. This allows for the retention of individuality as well as for the merging and compromising of certain cultural values which are close enough to each other to harmonize. However, children do not choose their parents nor their cultural backgrounds as individual spouses do. Thus, they are more likely to be vulnerable to develop symptoms of confusion, anxiety, depression, rebellion, and withdrawal if they are not able to accept and identify with the culture or even more complicated, *the cultures* into which they are born.

In our experience, intercultural marriages may be stable and work well until children enter the scene. At that point, compromises which have been worked out may not be sufficient to take care of new tasks and stresses as the family system reintegrates to include new children. In-law pressures are not necessarily required to produce conflicts over feeding, discipline, learning, and socialization. With the arrival of a child each spouse recalls memories of early childhood and attitudes, which become played out on the new infant as if they were a movie superimposed on another being shown on a screen. These recollections may have been buried for some time, and may not have played a significant role in the formation or early development of the marriage. However, when dormant feelings of early childhood are aroused, they can produce a new dimension of conflict in values between spouses, only to result in the child becoming the symptom of this conflict when he begins to display anxiety, rebellion, and difficulty learning in school or making friends.

Clinical Experience and a Research Project

To develop an understanding of the family dynamics associated with one culture, compared and contrasted to bicultural families, a family research program was conducted by the Department of Psychiatry. Families who sought psychiatric help because of emotional problems in one or more of their children were divided into three groups: those with two Caucasian parents; those with two Oriental parents from the same Oriental culture, and those with parents from two cultures, usually one Oriental and one Caucasian. (A detailed analysis of this study can be found in another report.) For the purposes of this chapter, we will focus on interactions in the third group of families (each parent is from a different culture) in which it appeared that their own conflicting attitudes toward child rearing contributed to the emotional problems in the youngster. While it is difficult to suggest a cause and effect relationship between culture conflict and emotional disturbance in the child, there are trends which suggest that risks in raising children can be minimized by parents from two different cultures if they are aware of them ahead of time, discuss them, and work out methods of coping with them.

Method

Briefly, each family in the larger research project participated in a standardized evaluation exercise in which the family was asked to create stories around a set of cards illustrating family scenes. The families were given as much time as they wanted and left alone to discuss each card. The families were videotaped throughout these discussions and also, individual biographical histories were gathered for the comparative study. The family interaction videotapes were analyzed. For the purpose of this discussion, we will focus on how the family members (children and parents) from intercultural marriages performed their various roles as parents and children, and how problems seen in this experimental laboratory situation might be considered to represent dysfunctional styles of interaction in a larger and more general sense. The microcosm of the videotaping session appeared to capture elements of behavior which reflected basic underlying attitudes and values of the parents which affected the child. (The validity of the videotaped sessions as representative of actual family life was verified. The exercise particularly focused upon those behaviors which appeared, in the laboratory setting, (1) to bring out the child's identified emotional difficulty, and (2) to clearly and visibly relate to cultural disharmony between the father and mother in their attempts to act as parents.) The majority of these families included

83

a Caucasian mother and an Oriental father. In most cases, Oriental parents were American born and raised in Hawaii but greatly influenced by the values of the Oriental communities in the state.

Results

Although there were many areas of positive functioning, enthusiastic cooperation, and exchange of ideas, nevertheless, various ways of taking turns, involving children in the story-telling task and certain conflicts between the parents surfaced. Several of the interactions observed were suggestive of culturally related models which were clung to, wittingly or unwittingly. In many instances, couples could not agree on the definitions of their respective parental roles. Some parents actively competed for family leadership, whereas others persistantly adhered to roles they thought appropriate in spite of their spouse's inability or reluctance to accept that role. For example, several Oriental husbands took a traditional role of standing and orchestrating the family situation (much as at a Chinese nine-course dinner a significant male in the family—not necessarily the father—stands and serves others sitting around the table). However, in many instances, Caucasian mothers repeatedly competed for this role, undercut their husbands, or attempted to act as co-leader with the husband. The husband might then ignore or reject her attempts to participate as an equal partner and include her in the task as one of the children. This "resolution" tended to produce withdrawal and mild symptoms of depression in the children, perhaps because of discouragement at witnessing the unsuccessful attempt at competition and assertiveness by one parent. In addition, the children in these instances felt excluded and unaccepted. On the other hand, when conflict continued between the husband and wife over the primary leadership role, the children tended to become restless, anxious, sometimes hyperactive and occasionally aggressive.

A second source of conflict between parents of interculturally married families was a difference between the parents' value systems. In several cases, parents placed a high premium on very different values and behaviors, such as creativity versus accuracy. One father instructed his children to limit their discussion strictly to the content of each picture. His wife, however, embellished on the content and urged the children to follow her example and use their imagination to tell more interesting stories. Because of this parental conflict, a general loss of creative ability was observed in the children. In addition, the children often became confused and disorganized because of the mixed messages sent to them resulting in inactivity or activity which was extremely cautious and guarded, as if the children felt a need to walk the tightrope between parental expectations and their own inclinations.

A third indication of conflict between parents was a tendency to avoid direct communication with one another by talking through their children. In most cases, one child, the youngster who was emotionally troubled, was singled out to receive the thoughts and ideas that actually were meant for the other spouse. One mother, who spoke very infrequently, directed all of her speech toward her son, never commented on her husband's story suggestions, and pointedly stated that her son's ideas were excellent. Her husband occasionally directed a comment toward his wife, but looked away and began talking to his son before she could respond. The son first exhibited anxiety and confusion at being considered an extension of each of his parents, or vehicle for their communication, or an alternate target for the spouse. Later, he tried another solution, that of responding to both parents, and finally attempted to focus their interest on the task itself in a desperately driven fashion without any pleasure or enjoyment in the task, in order to take the focus away from himself at all cost.

It was in this group of families that it was most evident that the child was an object of two different child rearing attitudes and appeared to suffer the most, finding no solution for the problem despite frantic attempts. In those families in which the dominant parents' perfectionist drive for precision was the strongest, children became angry by facial expression but could not discharge it, then became depressed at being unable to live up to unattainable standards, whether they related to one spouse's exaggerated emphasis on precision and accuracy, or the other's emphasis on creativity. In each case, it appeared that the struggle between the parents had exaggerated and distorted their predisposition toward a particular value and had thrust this upon the children who were unable to achieve it.

Adjustment Patterns Used to Resolve Parents' Cultural Differences

All couples bring to their marriages the cultures of their own nuclear families. If they share the same basic cultural background, their differences are usually minor and present few difficulties. As they live together, they gradually work out ways to deal with the differences. However, if they come from markedly different cultures, their differences may be more fundamental or complex. Thus, we will now focus on the adjustment patterns we have observed intermarried couples employ in attempting to resolve their differences and effect a synthesis of cultures so that a new harmonious "family culture" emerges. Some are more successful

85

than others. Success depends upon several factors: (1) the number and intensity of differences between a couple; (2) the kind of working agreement a couple employs in resolving differences; and (3) the level of satisfaction each spouse derives from that working agreement.

The adjustment couples make when they marry often encompasses a wide range of behaviors and values. Considered individually, each behavior or value may not seem immediately relevant to child development. However, as mentioned previously, the arrival of a child often brings to the surface unexpected values from the parents' own early years, values of an earlier generation, which may crystalize and clash. In addition, each consciously recognized cultural difference considered in the "personal" marriage pact, which goes beyond the legal binding of marriage, may not seem immediately relevant to child rearing. However, the total effect of many differences may later come to bear and significantly influence child-rearing in an unanticipated, exaggerated way. If the couple is not then able to resolve differences with quick and constructive working agreements, the number and intensity of these differences assumes even greater significance as the family grows.

Now, as one would deduce from the foregoing, there were a number of patterns by which couples in cross-cultural marriages sought to adjust their differences in this experiment. But, generally speaking, spouses from different cultures tended to seek solutions which related to the emotional or behavioral problems of their children, and some of these could be considered destructive and some constructive. We will now describe these patterns of adjustment. The first three fall in the category of destructive and the other two are constructive.

Destructive Patterns in Intercultural Marriages

Cold war adjustment. A cold war atmosphere characterized the adjustment pattern of some families. Parents in these families consistently emphasized different values and employed different approaches in working with their children. The parents never directly challenged or contradicted the spouse in, for example, leadership, but if the solution involved an alternate assumption of leadership, one spouse never actively participated in tasks when the other was supervising or disciplining children. As a result of the alternate leadership (but nonparticipation, alternating activity-passivity) as opposed to some combination in which mutual participation occurred, the children responded by following two different sets of instructions, became confused and easily distracted, producing very sketchy or fragmented stories. In actual life, such upset, of course, may produce difficulties in learning at school. Most cold war families functioned with difficulty since the stress of each change in leadership interrupted and often reversed the past performance, producing discontinuity rather than continuity in family functioning, and resulting in anxiety and confusion in the children.

In one family, the mother and father consistently employed different styles and emphasized different values. The mother enthusiastically engaged the children in telling stories, and tolerated boisterous behavior. Her husband sat passively and said nothing except for abruptly and periodically scolding the children for their disorderly behavior. At these moments, the mother immediately ceased talking and sat very still. When the father had finished lecturing, the children again became gradually disruptive under the mother's lack of direction. Each parent had passively agreed to tolerate the value system of the spouse, but insisted on adhering to his or her respective cultural values in a "time-sharing agreement." Although the couple's working process was not openly conflictual and permitted each parent to express his or her own values, it prevented them from working in concert and forced the children to cope with two inconsistent value systems. The parents were not unhappy with the disjointed quality of the family interaction even though it had an obvious adverse affect on the child who was anxious, confused, hyperactive, and highly sensitive to sudden changes in attitudes. One may conjecture that this pattern over an extended period would lead to difficulties in learning in school as well as rebellious behavior, regardless of standards, because of inability to integrate conflicting systems.

Competitive adjustment. Parents in the competitive adjustment category simultaneously competed for family leadership. In many cases, they emphasized the same values but competed strongly for the attention of their children. For example, when one father encouraged his son to notice the details of each picture card, the mother also quickly directed the boy to pay attention to detail. When the mother told the son to wait his turn before speaking, the father immediately began lecturing the boy about being polite and listening to others. Some parents even interrupted their children to debate certain points with their spouses. Parents raised their voices in competition and pressured their children to align with them and support their ideas. During the story-telling task of one family, each parent vigorously sought to seize family leadership. The parents frequently talked simultaneously until one of the children spoke, and then interrupted one another in response to the child. Each parent tended to counter the other parent's story suggestions with different interpretations of the pictures and urged the children to agree with their ideas. In some cases, it was commonly noted that mother and father shared common values regarding the behavior and intellectual development of their children. However, they did not agree on their respective child-rearing responsibilities. Often the father had married an Oriental woman expecting her to assume a less aggressive and supplementary role to his own leadership. However, he had also unwittingly involved himself heavily in areas traditionally reserved for women in the Orient, that is, child-rearing and domestic management. Unclear about their respective positions and family responsibilities, the parents engaged in a competitive working process and failed to resolve their primary unspoken differences. As a result of the parents' pitched battle, the one child who was very withdrawn at school and at home; his grades were poor because he refused to participate in any work that involved speaking. A possible conclusion is that where competition for leadership continues among spouses from different cultures, there is a risk that a child will become proportionately frightened, withdrawn, and depressed.

Reluctant adjustment. Both parents in this category were unwilling to act as the family's primary leader. In some cases, both parents were passive and allowed the children to influence family interaction at random. These families were either very disorganized or minimally organized. In other instances, only one parent in the family was passive; however, the spouse did not want to assume sole leadership. The active parent occasionally guided the family's task but waited unsuccessfully for the passive spouse to participate as a co-leader. Consequently, the child either received no guidance or suddenly received a limited amount of supervision and guidance from the active parent. Sometimes there was overt "spoiling" of a child by one parent as if the child was much younger.

The parents of one family formed a co-leader combination in which both were passive, either one comfortably assuming family leadership at alternate times. The children looked to their mother for guidance but she responded only when they complained loudly about one another or asked to leave the room. The father made almost no effort to supervise the family's performance and very rarely responded to his wife's request for support in directing the children to behave. He sat passively during most of task and occasionally held the baby when the mother handed it to him. One child continuously roamed about the room whining, while each of his older siblings told very long and belabored stories. The mother occasionally asked the older children if they would be finished with their stories soon but never actually set firm time limits on their stories. In most cases, the children decided when to conclude the stories and when to turn to a new one.

The only apparent discrepancy between the parents' values seemed to be their concepts of the parental role. Consequently, an effective working process failed to develop. The parents sat as reluctant observers of their children's behavior. The mother's obvious displeasure with the arrangement discomfitted the father. The child who was identified as the most emotionally troubled was characterized as very impulsive and defiant, unable to cooperate in school and hostile toward adults. There seemed to be a tendency in all the children either to compulsively assume an early premature pseudoadult control, or to be uncontrollably aggressive and disorganized. Each parent from a different culture had deferred to the other, leaving a vacuum for the children with no model or guidance.

Constructive Adjustment Patterns in Intercultural Marriages

The adjustment patterns that did appear to produce constructive family interaction in which the emotionally troubled child began to respond positively, were either designed by the parents as a result of their discovery of their part in the child's problem, or with the help of counseling. For our purposes, they are termed "complementary" and "additive."

Complementary adjustment. The roles of a complementary couple combined to provide the family with coordinated and consistent leadership. One parent assumed primary leadership duties while the spouse performed complementary parental functions. The family leader organized and moderated discussions. The spouse supported the leadership of the other, encouraged the children to participate, reinforced the leader's guidelines, and served as a model to the children by contributing to the task and listening to others.

For example, during one family's interview, the mother acted as the family leader, coordinating and stimulating the cooperation of the family in a task. The father assumed a supportive role, managing their active two-year-old, encouraging the older children, including one disturbed child, to help the mother tell stories, listening attentively to those who spoke and occasionally contributing an idea when the family couldn't think of one. The parents rarely communicated with one another orally or through eye contact, but worked together smoothly and involved the children in the task successfully as if an unconscious rhythm had developed between them. The mother was most concerned with stimulating the children intellectually and supporting their group efforts, while the father encouraged the children to behave properly and cooperate with their mother. In this case, the wife could express her own culturally assertive behavior in the constructive and receptive atmosphere of her husband's culture.

In most cases, complementary couples came from cultural backgrounds that shared similar views on parental roles and child rearing. In other cases, one of the parents decided to adopt the practices of the spouse's culture. Problems developed: (1) if a parent reluctantly accepted the spouse's culture and rejected his or her own; (2) if one parent became either extremely dominant or submissive; and (3) if the behavior of a parent did not coincide with the sex role assigned by the dominant culture of the extended family.

Additive adjustment. Parents in the additive adjustment category incorporated desirable qualities from each of their respective cultures and participated as equal partners in guiding the family's activities. For example, a Polynesian father and a Caucasian mother simultaneously emphasized the Caucasian value for high intellectual achievement and the Polynesian value for group cooperation. Throughout the task, both parents equally emphasized the two cultural values. As a result, the whole family worked together enthusiastically, trying to tell interesting stories. Leadership did not rest primarily with either parent but was undertaken jointly. The children accepted the joint leadership comfortably and the entire family worked together cooperatively.

Other successful additive adjustment may be achieved by blending positive attributes from two different cultures to develop a new interaction pattern. For example, the respective speaking styles of some Oriental and Caucasian cultures may be combined with constructive results. Japanese culture typically values subdued and comparatively unemotional speech, whereas Caucasian culture encourages more voluble and dynamic expressive behavior. By combining these speaking styles, one couple seemed to enrich their own communication and their family's interaction. The Oriental mother's quiet manner could discourage or curb loud and destructive arguments between family members and teach the children by example to use their emotions more effectively. The Caucasian father's expressive speaking style could stimulate interest in family discussions and encourage the children to express their own enthusiasm.

Conclusions and Summary

In this chapter, we have described intercultural family behavior styles (which were observed as part of a larger research project) to illustrate how a clash in cultural attitudes, values, and behaviors, either wittingly or unwittingly, produces emotional problems in children. Although parents may say that they agree in their approach to a child, their own attitudes toward one another actually are more important determinants.

The child will sense whether the parents respect one another and whether they are solidly together. Minor disagreements can occur but do not effect the basic relationship. Inconsistent or contradictory activity, in which one parent is permissive and the other overly strict, produces a family pattern in which there is no follow through. There are attempts to settle everything but nothing is settled. Punishments are threatened but not imposed; either that, or they are imposed and undone. Children consequently become confused, may try to take advantage of the situation through blackmail, manipulation, and tyranny. While these comments can apply to culturally homogeneous marriages, they reflect our clinical experience that they are high risk problems in cross-cultural marriages. That is, while they can be seen in the general population, they become exaggerated in their form and effect with the force of cultural differences behind them. Trends, usually reflected in the dominant parent, will now be spelled out more specifically. For example, the perfectionistic cold parent who comes from a background in which affection is not to be expressed and has difficulty expressing warmth, tends to impose many rules and regulations for children before they are ready. Overly strict and never satisfied, taking good work for granted and only noticing imperfection in a youngster's performance, unable to accept limitations and filled with exaggerated ambitions, that parent's background means that the parent demands so much of the child that the youngster decides he can never satisfy and gives up or enjoys opposing. Excessively rigid and punitive approaches which expect too much too soon in a form of adult-like conformity in small children tend to impose too many prohibitions at once rather than gradually at a pace the child can adapt to and understand. These excessively restrictive attitudes and expectations may force the child in one of two patterns: either chronic rebelliousness to get revenge on the parents, or into conformity and pseudomaturity. The "good" child becomes "good" at an enormous cost in personality growth, with constriction and narrowing of the range and potential for emotional expression. These children may end up as "perfect little ladies and gentlemen" or go to the other extreme, totally immune to severe punishment which has been used indiscriminately and inflexibly. Or, the child of the cold emotionally detached parent whose culture forbids the expression of warmth may become depressed and feel unloved and unaccepted, emotionally separated from the parent. These children may then enter a chronic state of rebellion against all rules and regulations, refusing to accede to adult demands, fighting back against a world whose rule they don't like and whose treatment has angered them.

Thus, chronic agression can come from two parental attitudes—too little love or too severe punishment. A third behavior pattern can also occur when a parent asks too much. The child may resort to passive resistance, agreeing but procrastinating. This behavior, stemming from too much demand, often extends into schoolwork where things just never get done. On the other hand, another cultural norm may allow for extreme and prolonged indulgence of children. The child who has been babied and not stimulated to assume an active role in mastering the world around him has so much gratification from prolonged infantile behavior that learning becomes too difficult and frustrating. The spoiled child never learns a relationship with authority and develops no values or standards of his own and has difficulty coping with the normal pressures of life. He may tyranize his parents and may appear very much like the children who are overdisciplined. That is, he may appear chronically rebellious, antagonistic, immature, and omnipotent because impulses have been given free reign. Or he may attempt to overcorrect himself because he becomes frightened of this loss of control and becomes contricted.

In summary, children with inner emotional immaturity have not outgrown earlier traits because of a lack of parental coordination, a dominant parent who is too lenient or too harsh, or inconsistent and competitive parents. The setting for child development is the family where the climate conditions the child's attitudes toward himself and others, in discovering and organizing the world around him.

Some intermarried families exhibited behavior patterns that differed from their own traditions. These new styles were an integration or synthesis of parts of the old, usually the most positive parts which allowed progressive growth of the family for its child-rearing task. The risk in marriage is that instead of this new synthesis, a clash between cultural styles will occur and affect the children adversely. However, when positive styles develop, they resulted in personality development in children which was not a half and half mixture of parental culture nor a rejection of one parental culture for the other, but a new and strong identity.

We, therefore, must conclude that part of marriage preparation and preparation for having children, especially when individuals from two differing cultures meet, should stress the importance of identifying particular cultural backgrounds of the intermarried individuals so that they will both be aware of the special difficulties likely to arise in child-rearing.

9
Adjustment in Intercultural Marriage

Wen-Shing Tseng, M.D.

A marriage is a process in which two persons learn to live together and adjust to each other in order to work toward common goals and achievements. When persons of different cultural backgrounds marry, because of the cultural factor their difficulties in adjusting to one another are far greater than for couples of the same culture. To the normal differences in personality, education, and life experience, must be added the differences in customs and values associated with differing cultures.

A successful marriage is not defined by the fact that it lasts a long time or does not end in divorce. The success of a marriage means that both husband and wife are well-integrated, working with each other harmoniously for the mutual satisfaction and achievement of common objectives. Therefore, subjectively both the husband and wife are happy and satisfied, and objectively they are well-adjusted and complement each other for a productive married life.

In order to attain these conditions of a successful marital adjustment, many qualities have been identified as essential. For example, each partner in the marriage must have some opportunity to express his or her own personality, must be an important focus of affection for the other, and must derive some pleasure and satisfaction from the marriage. These conditions, required for an ordinary marriage, must also exist for an intercultural marriage. However, if an intercultural marriage is defined as a union between two people who have divergent ways of life and backgrounds, then much extra effort must be expended.

Process of Cultural Adjustment

When two persons of different cultural backgrounds live together, certain adjustments usually occur as a result of the differences existing in their respective lives. These differences may appear to be very trivial, such as, how to celebrate a birthday, who is delegated to take out the garbage, or how to properly entertain a mother-in-law. On the other hand, there are very radical cultural differences, such as religion, social status of men and women, ownership of property, and child-rearing practices.

The processes of adjustment as discussed in this chapter do not imply that a particular intercultural marriage has to follow through certain chronological phases of adjustment, one by one. What it does mean is that there exist certain processes regarding each area of culture in which they are different, and that these must be resolved when the couple has been living together for some time.

When two people of different cultural backgrounds become acquainted, even though they may develop affection for each other and establish mutual interests, sooner or later they will begin to discover that some kinds of differences exist between them. While they are dating each other, they may be aware of the existence of such differences but may not really realize how seriously the differences could affect their lives until they begin living together. An illustration can be seen when a Caucasian who considers potatoes to be an essential part of a decent meal marries an Oriental who eats rice with every meal. This difference may seem trivial but can become a problem when the couple must eat the same foods at the same meal.

The issue of the place of marriage may not occur to the couple until the planning of the wedding. Suddenly they may realize that they have a serious problem. It is very important for the Oriental male to have the wedding ceremony and party planned and organized by the groom's parents in order to show that the woman is marrying "into" the husband's house. The Caucasian female very often insists that it is important for her family to arrange the wedding, as this has long been the custom in her society.

Before two persons from different cultures marry, they are quite likely to think of one another in a stereotyped manner. After marriage, the difference between fantasy and reality becomes apparent. Take, for example, the not untypical example of an American soldier marrying a Southeast Asian girl while still overseas. Both of them are likely to have notions about one another that are wide of the mark. The girl may well believe that all Americans are rich, own fine cars, and live in palatial homes.

However, when she reaches the United States, she may discover that her soldier husband is anything but rich and propertied. By the same token, the husband may have married the girl under the mistaken notion that all Oriental girls are submissive and wait hand and foot on their husbands. He quickly discovers differently.

This type of discovery and recognition of differences does not occur only during the initial stage of marriage but may continue even after the couple has lived together for many years. Marriage is a process of developing events which the couple encounters and continually faces and they must adjust to the new tasks or problems and also discover the new differences that exist between them. This is particularly true concerning certain life events such as weddings, births of children, buying of property, and funerals. Partners in an intercultural marriage react according to their cultural backgrounds and sometimes cultural differences can be troublesome. For example, a happily intermarried couple after several years of marriage may have a baby. What to name the child, whether or not it should be baptized and how to celebrate the birth are serious questions which may arise as a result of their differing cultural backgrounds. Another type of situation which may occur after years of marriage is the death of a Chinese parent. The non-Chinese wife is expected to follow the Chinese tradition of honoring the dead parent at the funeral ceremony. However, it is against her religion to "worship" ancestors and she does not feel that she should have to do this. Obviously, a cultural conflict is created in this situation within the intercultural marriage.

Many people are so unprepared to accept these differences that they frequently experience a feeling of strangeness and isolation, each feeling like an outsider. When one of the partners does not know how to react to a particular situation in which a particular behavior is expected, it can create a problem. In the Orient, cousins of the opposite sex do not show physical affection toward each other. Therefore, the Oriental husband is confused when meeting his American wife's relatives for the first time and finds that she is physically affectionate to all her relatives, including her male cousins. He does not know how to behave. Conversely, when the American wife meets the parents of her Oriental husband and receives only a handshake, she may feel rejected if she does not realize that this is an appropriate and warm reception for their daughter-in-law.

Very frequently, a person will not be able to perceive or recognize the existence of the cultural difference. He will react to a situation from his own cultural point of view, not knowing that his partner is behaving according to another cultural system of values. For example, a young American wife may become very angry and frustrated when her Chinese husband does not give her a birthday gift on her first birthday after their marriage. She is accustomed to sending and receiving presents and cards on birthdays and naturally becomes upset when her birthday is not remembered by a present or even a card from her husband. The husband does not understand why she cries and carries on over this matter. Neither partner can see the situation from the other cultural point of view.

In order to deal with the disorientation caused by the initial encounter, a couple begins to speculate on the reasons for their differences and possible solutions. To illustrate, a.newly married husband places his shoes outside the bedroom door. In his culture, this means that his wife is supposed to shine the shoes for him. She, however, does not understand this custom and, therefore, does not perform according to his expectations. When he sees that his shoes have not been shined, he becomes angry and she does not know why. It may take several days for this unfortunate wife to discover that the reason her husband has been angry has something to do with the shoes. A couple must be aware of potential misunderstandings that can occur. Each partner must make an extra effort to check the meaning of the other's actions and words. If the channels of communication can be opened regarding the confused matter in this case, soon the wife may learn from her husband that, according to his culture, it is very important for the wife to shine her husband's shoes. This is a way of demonstrating her willingness to be a "dutiful" wife to her husband, and it will make the man feel that he, as an "important and respected" man, is served by his wife. Actually, after they discuss this matter, she may learn that he is willing to do chores around the house and doesn't expect to be "served" all of the time, but he does want her to behave as a "dutiful" wife in front of his mother.

It is essential that the two people can sit down and begin to talk about their motivations—why he did this, why she feels that way—and how these are due to individual needs, family customs, or cultural patterns. Then the couple will be in a better position to reach a solution to the difference. If the Oriental husband realizes that for his American wife a birthday is a day for her to enjoy privileges and to be entertained, he might be willing to go along with her on this subject. The wife might also realize that the husband's culture regards birthday celebrations as appropriate only for very small children and older parents as a sign of respectful filial-parent behavior. Through an attitude of mutual understanding, each partner may try to reinterpret the other's actions from their cultural point of view, and thus a new problem-solving pattern may emerge.

Any problems or differences which may exist within an intercultural marriage will not be solved easily just because cognitively the persons are aware of the reason for the difference and strategically there is a prescribed solution for it. Culture is something which is learned through experiences in early life. An individual has developed strong emotional attachments to his culture—associated with his belief system, values, and habits—his style of life. In the process of intercultural marriage adjustment, he has to learn how to overcome, correct, and adjust his emotional reaction to the necessary change and expansion of his cultural behavior. Since an individual has developed a set system of emotions associated with a set of behaviors, it usually takes a great deal of work and time to readjust. If, in the past, he felt that it was shameful and embarrassing to show physical affection to his spouse in public, he now has to learn that it is positive behavior and to feel that it is a proud and comfortable action. It is not only a matter of replacing the old feeling with the new feeling, but also of reacting almost in a 180 degree reverse manner. It is necessary to work on the matter of resistance and complication which may occur in association with his process of rearranging his pattern of emotional response. For instance, an American husband, conservatively raised, who marries a Micronesian wife and stays in Micronesia, has to learn to feel comfortable watching his wife expose her breasts in public as the other women do in her native land. Although he cognitively understands that this practice is customary and that the native husbands do not object, emotionally he cannot accept it. He must find some way to accept this cultural difference in such a way that he can feel comfortable with it.

As another example, a Chinese wife may use her own chopsticks to pass and serve food to family members and guests because to her this is a way of showing kindness, graciousness, intimacy, and respect. However, her Japanese husband considers this use of chopsticks as "dirty" and disrespectful. In his culture, everyone uses his own bowl and chopsticks, and never transfers food from one person to another with chopsticks. Actually, it is quite a taboo to do it since in the Japanese funeral ceremony the chopsticks are used to transfer the bones of the dead from the monk to the family member. Thus, he cannot accept her custom emotionally, although cognitively he realizes the differences in their cultural practices.

Since the process for such adjustments involves deep feelings, it is better not to hurry the change in emotional behavior, as it may destroy the equilibrium in the mind and produce unexpected complications. It is better to allow the person to have the time to try and then to retry, so that he will feel comfortable and become more natural in showing the new response emotionally. In the process of changing his emotional behavior from the old to the new, it is very helpful to sometimes provide the opportunity of "time out," so that the person does not feel overly exhausted in trying the new behavior pattern.

The most desirable state to be reached in the process of cultural adjustment is the final achievement of balance. In this condition, a person discovers and appreciates the value of both cultures, accepts the difference which may exist between himself and his spouse without discomfort, and is also willing to try new behavior for the purpose of new adjustment with the greatest possible flexibility. In this condition, he feels confident about the possible outcome, knowing that certain kinds of solutions can always be achieved and feels ready to face any situation which may be encountered. Through experience, the couple has already established certain guidelines for the negotiation of any difference that may exist between them. Therefore, they can spontaneously know when, where, and in what circumstances to behave in accordance with each culture. An achievement of this quality is essential to a successful adjustment.

Patterns of Intercultural Adjustment

When two people of divergently different cultural backgrounds encounter one another, theoretically there may occur several patterns of solution within their cultural adjustment to one another.

Regarding one aspect of the cultural behavior, such as language, religion, foods, or social activities, a person may give up his own original cultural behavior and take on the custom of the spouse—so-called "one-way adjustment." This is one type of solution that can occur. There are several possible reasons for this one-way adjustment. One aspect of a culture may be so dominant that it strongly demands everything be done according to that custom. For example, some religions demand that the spouse convert to that religion. The same may apply to language; a group may be extremely proud of its language and insist upon using it instead of another. This is determined by the dominance of the culture.

In the same way, but separated from the culture, such a one-way adjustment may occur if one of the spouses has a very strong personality, and insists that things be done in his or her way. If the husband strongly feels that it is important to have a sports car, the wife may have to comply with his wishes to purchase it. Or, if the wife insists it is very important to have her own bank account, he will probably comply with her desire.

Another reason for this type of adjustment is that it may be more practical for everyday life. For example, it is very practical when living in the

United States for the Oriental wife to learn to drive a car and shop in a supermarket; on the other hand, many American wives would be happy to have a maid while living in an Asian country where maids are easily available. A person may give up his original cultural behavior not in order to adopt a new one but because he does not have strong feelings toward his own, or possibly even has negative feelings.

Regarding such one-way adjustment, it is not so much the particular meaning—implication of good or bad, right or wrong—but the underlying reason for making such a "one-way" adjustment that is important. A human life is a constant process of change or improvement; we all have to give up some old habits and learn new. A total capitulation to the other culture, however, with complete abolishment of one's own background and behavior, can indicate poor cultural identification originally and a pathological relationship between the dominant member and the submissive one.

The second type of adjustment is to practice the culture behavior of both partners in an alternating way—sometimes trying the husband's way, sometimes the wife's way. The "alternative adjustment" may occur because both of the spouses insist that their cultural behavior be observed and there is no way of giving up either one, or of mixing them. Therefore, they have decided to follow certain customs at one time and others at another time. For example, it may be very difficult for a couple to have the kind of ceremony that would meet the religious requirements of both sides. However, it would be very possible to have a Catholic wedding in the morning and a Buddhist one in the afternoon, satisfying the cultural requirements of both persons. Similarly, for a couple from Jewish and Protestant backgrounds a church wedding and one in a synagogue could both be held. In these cases, no emotional conflict is involved, and both cultural traditions are observed.

Another reason for this kind of adjustment is the fact that both partners appreciate each other's life patterns, habits, and needs, so that they enjoy a variety of lifestyles and can alternate them. An example of this can be seen in the serving of foods in the household. It is a relatively easy matter to serve hamburgers or steak one day, and shrimp tempura and sashimi with rice the next. Another example is to have a Christmas tree and presents on Christmas day in order to make the Christian wife happy, and a New Year gift and celebration to satisfy the Oriental husband. There is no conflict and each enjoys his own and the other's customs.

A variation of this type of problem solution pattern is the "simultaneous" solution, in which both cultures are adopted in certain situations, and are comfortably combined. Such would be the case with a Chinese husband who was ill and chose to consult a modern Western physician for his ailment, while also consulting with a practitioner of traditional Chinese medicine.

A "mid-point compromise" is the type of solution most appropriately used in a quantitatively measurable situation. For example, a Chinese husband may feel required to send a hundred dollars per month to support his elderly parents out of filial respect; his American wife may feel that their own nuclear family cannot spare the money and that his parents should take care of themselves. When each realizes the other's position in light of the different cultural backgrounds and customs, they may agree to send only fifty dollars per month for this purpose.

Another example would concern the number of children to have in a family. The husband may come from a culture which greatly emphasizes having a large family, and therefore he may wish to have many children to make himself feel masculine. The wife, who comes from a culture which does not stress having many children, and in fact would prefer to have only one or two children, may feel that it is too much of a burden and that this would mean her only purpose in life would be to bear children. This couple may choose a mid-point compromise regarding the number of children so that somehow both meet each other's needs.

Most issues, even though accompanied by individual ideas or feelings, can be expressed, discussed, and dealt with by choosing some mid-point compromise. The most significant matter is the attitude behind this, the willingness to respect each other's needs and to make the effort to compromise in order that both individuals feel satisfied.

Perhaps one of the most frequent methods chosen for the intercultural adjustment is "mixing." A concrete example would be a wedding between a Hawaiian and a Japanese—possibly having a Shinto-style ceremony with Hawaiian music and flower leis, and entertaining the guests with Japanese sake and a Hawaiian luau. The couple's home may be a combination of a Western-style building utilizing Japanese *shoji* doors, decorated with Hawaiian tapa wall hangings, set in a Japanese garden.

In such a mixed manner of adjustment, every part may be taken randomly so that the total picture looks very awkward, or carefully and wisely selected and combined so that it is harmonious, balanced, well-matched, and creates a new kind of beauty. Even though such a mixing can be observed in concrete matters such as dressing, housing, or religious behavior, it also occurs in the behaviors of couples on the level of concepts and ideas.

A "creative adjustment" takes place when both partners decide to give up the cultural behavior of both sides and invent a completely new behavior pattern. The reason may be that they are not particularly satisfied with their own cultural behavior nor happy with the others, so this stimuates both to create a new pattern to meet their needs. For example, they are not happy about being married in the church according to the Christian custom nor do they want a traditional ceremony at home. Therefore, they decide to marry in a unique way—in an airplane or on the beach.

Sometimes this method of solution is chosen because there is too much conflict or competition existing between both cultural patterns and there is little chance for negotiation. Therefore, trying a completely new way will avoid such confrontations. Sometimes this phenomena occurs because the two cultural behaviors are not only different but conflicting; one is insulting to the other. Then it is necessary to try a third one even in a very random way. According to Western customs the ladies are seated at a table first, followed by the gentlemen. The guest of honor sits next to the hostess, with males and females alternating around the table. In the Oriental way, the age and social status of the guests become the primary concerns of how to seat them at the table. Definitely, the men come first and the ladies second. The room is a major concern. The guest of honor sits in the uppermost position, furthest from the door, while the host and hostess sit in the lower position—near the door and furthest away from the honored guest. Because of such a different system of etiquette, to follow any one aspect of it may eventually insult the guests of the other culture. Therefore, it is very difficult to follow any one custom if there is a mixture of guests from both cultures. One solution may be to create a new system—asking the guests to sit randomly.

Factors Contributed to Successful Adjustment

Even though intercultural marriage is defined as a marriage between two persons of different cultural backgrounds who hypothetically need more effort to adjust to each other in their relationship, many people are very successful in such an adjustment. There are several factors which are essential for such success.

The concept of marriage may be different in different societies and vary at different times. Nevertheless, the elemental nature of marriage is that a man and woman who are fond of each other decide to live together for the mutual goal of forming a family to stabilize and improve the quality of their life. If a couple gets married for this purpose, we consider this as a sound motivation. However, sometimes people get married for other reasons, resulting in a so-called "neurotic marriage." For example, a person may get married simply for material benefit, or just to escape from his original home. This is not only true for the ordinary marriage, but also true for some intercultural marriages. For an Asian girl to marry an American GI as a way of getting a ticket to leave her country, or for a black man to marry a white woman and mistreat her to gratify his resentment toward white people are examples of so-called "neurotic" motivations. These are not likely to end in happy marriages. To demand certain conditions for marriage is another example of neurotic motivation. A Chinese husband may insist that his American wife have a male child as a condition for getting married, or the American wife may insist that their child be given her Western family name. All such situations are likely to create conflict rather than lead to a harmonious married life. Therefore, the motivation for the marriage should be as sound as possible.

Since so many changes and adjustments have to be achieved in the process of marriage, particularly for the intercultural marriage, it is very important that the couple is open minded enough to see that many other ways of living exist in the world, and is willing to try new things and to make changes if necessary, instead of being rigid and resistant to change. A high tolerance for confusion, an acceptance of areas of dissatisfaction, and a knowledge of how to appropriately change one's attitude according to the situations are equally important. All these qualities are essential for any kind of marriage, but again, they are very important in intercultural marriage.

Since the marriage depends on the two people rather than on the individual, it is very important that these two people should be a good match in terms of sensitivity to the other's needs. They need to realize that differences will always occur in the periphery of life but that a basically similar centrality of thought about life is held between them, and that they have a mutual consideration of what is important to the other, respect each other's point of view and have an attitude of "fairness" for both. The most important thing is that they share a common goal, toward which they are strongly motivated.

The environment, which affects our life in the visible and nonvisible way in many respects, becomes relatively crucial for the intercultural marriage. If the community tends to accept the intercultural marriage with little discrimination, then it will be a lot easier for the couple to live in that setting, to make friends, and have a satisfying social life. It is particularly important, while they are raising children, to see that their children are well accepted by the neighborhood, school, and peer group.

Even though the nuclear family is the popular style of life in contemporary society, the family of both sides still has a lot of imput to the marriage, not only in actuality, but also at the psychological level. Many couples face conflict and crisis whenever the family of either side visits them or stays with them even for a very short period of time. It is a time for them to decide how to behave or react according to which family custom or which cultural behavior, and very likely they are forced to confront each other more often regarding their differences. It is very important that the marriage be accepted and supported from both sides of the family so that differences will be minimized.

Even though the marriage should be considered as a process of adjustment to each other, it is also very useful from time to time for the spouse to have a temporary "vacation" in which to return to his own lifestyle so that he/she will be ready to make other new adjustments. Such a vacation does not necessarily mean a return to his/her homeland to meet people of the same group, but can be a time to be able to think, behave, and feel according to the way he/she used to.

The Positive Aspect of Intercultural Marriage

In the past, intercultural marriage tended to be conceptualized as a marriage with potential problems and difficulties in adjustment. A positive aspect has been neglected if we assume that our life is a continuous process of change and improvement, not only originating from the inside but also from contact with and stimulation from the outside; thus, intercultural marriage should be considered as a means of bringing in new stimuli from the outside, and also as a challenging way of introducing adjustments. Actually, the couples who intermarry may be considered pioneers who are brave enough to allow adventure into their lives by breaking the traditional patterns. Those couples who intermarry even against possible resistance and succeed in overcoming problems, have strong common goals, act as a positive balance to each other, and have the ability to adjust. Thus, the successful intercultural marriage should be considered a good example of masterful intercultural adjustment.

10
Intercultural Marriages: Problems and Challenges for Psychiatric Treatment

J. David Kinzie, M.D.

When a patient comes for psychiatric treatment, the therapists need to ask about the patient's relationship with his wife, husband, boyfriend, or girlfriend, as these relationships are often extremely important in the formulation and treatment of an individual. Additionally, many times the relationship itself is the problem and needs to be the focal point of the treatment. When patients or couples appear for psychiatric help, but are from different cultural backgrounds, there are added problems and challenges for psychiatric treatment. The goals of this chapter are to describe an approach to intercultural marriage; to offer a method of analyzing the effects of culture and ethnic factors on the presenting symptoms; and to give some techniques for the therapy of these problems.

In the analysis of everyday problems in living, or complex psychopathology, it is obvious that complicated factors, such as early life experiences, biological and genetic factors, stress, and sociocultural influences, interact to give the presenting picture. The case is even more complicated with a patient who presents with a psychiatric problem, and whose mate is from another cultural background. Therefore, I feel the approach requires increasing clinical competence in dealing with this group in which cultural factors, as well as the relationship itself, need to be analyzed within the framework of the patient's own life. Clinical competence implies that the therapist takes a complete history and the appropriate mental status examination on one or both members of the marriage if they are available. Additionally, it is important to take a cultural history from each partner. This involves questioning the type of family the patient came from; the models the parents set; the roles of the father and mother; the communication styles within the family; the attitudes in the family towards religion; their display of emotions and affection; the family or cultural values placed on marriage, work, future; the ongoing type of obligations and relationships to the nuclear family; the goals and expectations each had from their marriage; and the family's attitudes about the marriage. Particularly important is the discussion of each partner as well as their family's attitude about seeing a psychiatrist or a therapist. These questions should be asked in addition to questions about the usual problems encountered in family therapy, about current problems, about their ability to communicate with their partners about their problems, and the feelings they have about these problems.

As with all cross-cultural types of psychotherapy, it is important for the therapist to remember his own value systems so that he can control his unconscious reactions to one partner or another. In addition, his own style of relating and of therapy may offend or be inappropriate to one or both of the partners that he is working with. For example, an outspoken, "tell-it-like-it-is" therapist may come on so strong that he intimidates a member of a particular ethnic group because his style is so foreign to that individual. He then may be unable to correctly identify the interaction between the couple, and may either correctly or mistakenly identify as an immediate ally of one side of the relationship. On the other hand, the therapist may quickly overidentify with one partner, such as an apparently quiet, submissive spouse, and feel a need to protect or completely miss the other aspects of the communication that this person gives. An awareness of the therapist's own values and style, and flexibility in using that style is extremely important in being helpful with a cross-cultural couple.

With private patients, as well as with supervision of a large number of patients under residents' care, the problems encountered in interculturally married patients who come for psychiatric treatment, are of three types.

In the first group are those couples to whom the difference in cultures and/or ethnic factors are not important in the analysis or treatment of the case and therefore treatment can be directed along usual lines of therapy.

The second group are those patients in whom cultural factors obscure or complicate the usual treatment methods for one or another of the partners. Here the cultural factors are not themselves a factor in the problem, but make analysis and treatment more difficult.

In the third group cultural factors contribute directly to the conflict or marital problems. Here therapeutic intervention must consider these cultural differences as directly relating to the problem.

This rather simple framework is not meant to imply that these factors are operating all the time in any couple, but that at any one time cultural factors may not be important, or may complicate the therapy, or may be the primary importance of the therapy, while that would not be true at another point in time with the same couple.

Interculturally Married Couples to Whom Differing Cultural Backgrounds Present No Problems in Treatment

In one case, the patient is a 51-year-old Hawaiian female, married to a 55-year-old Caucasian male. She entered the hospital with toxic organic brain symptoms, secondary to steroid therapy for systemic lupus disease. Her symptoms were of agitation and of confusion, included hallucinations and delusions involving some Hawaiian themes referring to Hawaiian royalty, and her speech used a great deal of Hawaiian words and phrases often without benefit of translation. Her husband was a devoted man who had helped her during her chronic illness a great deal. He probably had been over solicitous and had encouraged her dependency, but this was not markedly out of keeping with her disability. She responded well to psychiatric treatment, and although her posthospital course was quite prolonged, she eventually recovered a great deal of her previous functioning ability. The husband continued to be involved in most aspects of the treatment and was able to encourage her to do more work, and gave her more responsibility as she improved. She continued to occasionally use Hawaiian terms but quickly gave an English equivalent expression, but otherwise had no other obvious cultural incongruities with her husband.

In this case, which had more obviously an organic etiology, the wife's background was from a different culture than her husband's. However, they seemed to have long ago resolved the differences that existed and functioned well without cultural factors seeming to be important in the treatment or outcome of the case. The culturally colored delusions were only incidental to the primary problem and would be inappropriate for detailed analysis while the toxic psychosis remained untreated.

In another instance, the patient is a mid-twenty-year-old girl, of Hawaiian and second generation Filipino ancestry. She presented after having many legal problems associated with a compulsive need to steal and to exaggerate her life circumstances. She had kept these activities secret from her husband, a man of Caucasian-Japanese background. She was very reluctant to discuss them with him for fear that he would leave her or beat her, as in fact, her own father had done. However, once he was brought into the therapy, he displayed a great deal of tolerance and understanding for her behavior, took appropriate steps with the financial problems, and became more involved in her own personal finances. With him present, she was able to recount a great deal of her background, in which she, with her mother's approval, was able to control a dominating father by sly and devious tactics.

Although the couple came from different cultural and socioeconomic backgrounds, the patient's central problem was related to her own past and relationships within her family. However, she and her husband had a basically healthy relationship. The patient learned that when problems did occur, she was able to discuss them with her husband. Insight and ventilation with restructuring of the family relationship proved to be valuable techniques.

Cultural Factors Which Obscure or Complicate the Usual Treatment and Method for One Partner of Intercultural Marriage

The first example concerns a 50-year-old Caucasian male married to a second generation Japanese woman. He came because of their difficulties in handling a teenager who had increasing numbers of school problems, and who had been somewhat rebellious at home. It was originally suggested in therapy that his wife join him, as well as, perhaps, other family members, in handling this problem. His wife, however, did not approve of seeing a psychiatrist, feeling that the family problems were too personal to discuss with an outsider. Treatment then was directed at the patient and his relationship with both the children and the wife. It was determined that many of the problems which were apparently of a communication nature, were actually not as difficult as had been imagined. The patient and therapist both began to realize that the couple communicated very well, albeit in a nonverbal, indirect manner. In fact, the patient became aware that he and his wife had a strong complementary family. Using the communication skill he had learned for indirect communication in his family, things seemed to markedly improve, between he and his wife and the children.

Here is one case in which the cultural preference of one partner, (that is,) the Japanese wife who did not want to discuss family problems with a psychiatrist and who used indirect and subtle means of communication, complicated a treatment setting in which family therapy would be the usual expected mode of treatment. However, this did not prevent some progress from being made and the therapist from learning that the family, in fact, was functioning well, and that there were means by which the husband and wife could communicate, although perhaps not as directly as the husband would have liked.

The second example deals with a 30-year-old female patient, born and raised in Western Europe. She married a local, second generation Hawaiian-Japanese, when he was stationed in Europe. She had an acute schizophrenic break, with severe social withdrawal and delusions. The husband dutifully visited her in the hospital, and was always available for the psychiatrist conferences and interviews. When it became obvious that some of the problems the wife faced were due to his overwork, unattentiveness, lack of expression, and continued family obligations, it was suggested that family therapy between them be initiated as part of ongoing outpatient treatment. The husband agreed to this and did, in fact, attend several sessions. However, he continued to be shy and taciturn, obedient and obsequious, in relating to the therapist. He said very little of a meaningful nature, and nodded respectfully, if not enthusiastically with the suggestions for more communications in the family setting. When it was later suggested that this lack of adequate communication presented some difficulty in the wife's expectations of the marriage, they terminated family therapy, although she continued to be seen periodically, and in fact had subsequent hospitalization.

This patient had schizophrenic attacks which were probably only partially precipitated due to the marital problems. However, the marital problems which centered around large cultural differences in their expectations of marriage, ongoing obligations to family, and communication styles, as well as displays of emotion, complicated the treatment. The husband's style of relating to a professional continued to make marital therapy difficult. On the other hand, he continued to be involved with medical aspects of her treatment such as medication and outpatient visits for her. This couple was able to work directly at the medical problem involved in acute schizophrenia, but were unable to work on the marital problems, since they seemed so difficult for them to handle.

Another couple involved a Caucasian male in his late twenties, and a similarly aged Chinese-Hawaiian female. They consulted a therapist because over the past several months their relationship seemed more strained, and the wife was described as cold and distant. In addition, both of them described her renewed interest in her Hawaiian background, and her search for Hawaiian roots and her need to become a leader of the Hawaiian people. This was interpreted by both the original therapist and a consulting psychiatrist as her need to find her own identity in the framework of her minority group status. Eventually, however, the behavior seemed more unusual in that even though she was only one fourth Hawaiian she insisted that she look for her own Hawaiian burial ground on a neighbor island, and revealed that she had had a secret message that she was a leader of Hawaiian people, and that other aspects of her life showed further ideas of reference and delusions. Further history, which the husband then revealed, was that she had periods of staring, posturing, and noncommunicating, as well as an erratic social life for the past three months. Subsequent history confirmed that she was undergoing a schizophrenic attack, and her behavior became more bizarre, erratic, and unpredictable. She refused treatment, left her family, and moved from the area.

This patient represents a person undergoing a serious mental illness, whose symptoms were first accepted as a cultural variation, and a need to find her own identity and roots within her culture. A search for background and culture symbols was accepted for a time by her husband, her family, and the therapist as legitimate growth experience. However, the cultural coloring of the symptoms prevented detection of a severe disorder, obscured and eventually prevented the treatment of a serious psychiatric illness.

Cultural Factors Which Contribute Directly to the Conflict or the Marital Problem of a Couple in their Relationship

In this case, the patient is a mid-30-year-old Hawaiian male, married to a Caucasian female. He has a history of explosive attacks, often associated with alcohol consumption, which had cost him several jobs in past, and some hospitalization. The explosive outbursts were controlled with medication, and psychotherapy aimed at finding different ways of expressing himself. However, the marital problem became evident as his other symptoms subsided. The patient came from a violence-prone home where there was very little verbal communication, and any disruption of the alcoholic father's routine was met with immediate physical punishment. On the other hand, the wife came from a loud, verbally aggressive home, where there was no display of physical aggression. It became evident during the couple's therapy that neither side could understand the communication styles which they had grown up with in their own homes. The husband could not imagine a family where people could yell at each other and yet not physically be aggressive, and where there was genuine love displayed at other times. The wife, on the other hand, could not understand a family where every disagreement ended in a physical confrontation. Despite ongoing analysis of family styles, types of communication, as well as personal experiences that each had had, the ongoing conflict was extremely difficult to dislodge.

The culture values here may be more idiosyncratic in the sense of representing a personal family style rather than the more ubiquitous Caucasian or Hawaiian style. However, the attitudes ingrown in the families directly affected the relationship in an ongoing way and represented marked difficulty in eliminating or compromising the more disruptive aspect of their relationship.

For example, one patient is a 30-year-old Caucasian female, divorced and working as a physician's assistant. She has been living for one year with a Hawaiian male construction worker, who was currently unemployed due to chronic back pain. Only after some months of living together did she apparently recognize he was abusing drugs, allegedly for his pain. Additionally, she was upset by his leaving for long periods of time, not talking to her, threatening violence when the situation became tense, and by apparently taking her for granted. She however was attracted by his physical strength, his fun-loving attitude when he was feeling good, and by involvement in the extended family in which she was readily accepted. The patient felt that the conflicts she was experiencing were cultural, and later realized that many of them were directly related to her superior use of language, which was often used in a sarcastic and demanding way. She learned to accept some of his styles of relating, was able to find ways of expressing herself nonverbally, and to accept his expressions of affection, which were generally nonverbal. The relationship seemed to be more comprehensible to her, if not entirely satisfactory.

This case represents marked contrast in both personal styles and cultural values, so much so that one wonders at times how couples who are so different get together. However, aside from their differences in social class, educational level, and previous training , there were also cultural differences reflected in their attitudes about such basic values as the meaning of relationship, communication styles, the role of an extended family, perhaps even the role of men and women within the relationship. Although the couple was not seen in couples therapy, she did gain some insight into her way of communicating as well as into his, and was able to avoid the more threatening forms of confrontation. She was also able to sort out the problems she personally encountered in relationships versus those which are inherent in a relationship when people come from such different backgrounds.

In another case, the couple is twenty-year-old second generation Okinawan boy, and his girlfriend, a nineteen-year-old Japanese-Filipino female. They have been living together for six months and plan to get married within the next year. They were seen individually for personal problems; he with a disassociated episode, and she with tension headaches and anxiety attacks. However, it became obvious to both that the relationship was a source of much of their problems. He was raised in a traditional family and had more recently discovered some of the past roots of his heritage, which included a revived interest in Buddhist shrines and his ancestors. Also as oldest son, he felt a certain obligation to continue family ties, frequently visited home, and gave part of his own income to his family. Emotions were rarely expressed in the family, and his own life seemed to be a very quiet, unexpressive one. The girl's background was quite different, although in theory the part-Japanese cultural origins related with some similarity to her boyfriend's background. However, her family was more Americanized in their values. The patient and her mother talked a great deal about their personal lives to each other several serious relationships with men, as well as a large circle of outside friends. She appeared to be more verbally aggressive, and at times even explosive, in her relationships. She was extremely disturbed by his continued attachment to his family, by his frequent visits home, by his seemingly placing affection to his family before her. She tended to react strongly to these flights in their relationship and her manner tended to drive him away from her even more. She had serious doubts about this being the right boy for her and their marriage was on the verge of being called off.

Despite an apparent cultural similarity, that is, Okinawan and part-Japanese, the patients both came from markedly different backgrounds. The attachment to the family, the obligation of the older son, and his own quiet limited verbal interaction, caused a great many problems for both him and for her, which were exacerbated by her tendency to verbal emotional displays. Despite their own similar analysis of the situation, they were reluctant to be counseled together, which probably was associated with her doubts about the relationship which she did not want to express to him, and his own method of not relating emotions or feelings in her presence. Cultural conflicts here seem central to the relationship; at the same time, the personal as well as cultural conflicts prevented them from seeking help together.

In conclusion, patients with intercultural marriages who request psychiatric treatment present many challenges to the treating therapist. In addition to being clinically competent in handling the the usual range of psychopathology, he must be able to take from each partner a cultural history involving beliefs, values, early family life, family communication styles, models provided by parents, and expectations of marriage. After a thorough history a determination usually can be made if the cultural factors are incidental to the primary problem, complicate or obscure the primary problem or are directly involved as the primary problem. This analysis thus allows treatment to be directed toward the primary difficulty and avoids focusing upon cultural themes which may be irrelevant to the case. In cross-cultural therapy it is important for the therapist to be aware of his own value system and not react unconsciously to one partner or the other. He needs to be open-minded and as clearly as possible listen to each side. It is imporant for the therapist to take the patients with the situation as it presents itself. This means flexibility in approaches even to the point of working with a patient whose partner, because of culturally induced attitude, will not seek psychiatric help.

11
Intercultural Marriages under Stress: The Effect of Chronic Illness

Jon Streltzer, M.D.

In-depth studies of intercultural marriages may reveal the effect of different cultural backgrounds on the dynamics of the marriage. However, generalizations from individual case studies are risky at best. It would be tempting to say that there are no generalizations that can be made about intercultural marriages; that intercultural marriages are fundamentally the same as homocultural marriages; that the type of relationship that occurs and the relative success or failure of the marriage relate primarily to the dynamics occurring between the two individuals. On the other hand, without assuming that culture is of primary importance in the marriage, it is legitimate to question whether an intercultural marriage is advantageous or disadvantageous; whether some cultural mixes tend to work better than others; whether intercultural marriages present an advantage or disadvantage in raising children, functioning as husband and wife, or coping with the stresses of daily life.

One method of approaching these questions would be to compare large groups of intercultural marriages with homocultural marriages. In order for the comparison to be meaningful, these groups would have to be well matched on all characteristics other than culture; that is, they would need to be similar in regard to age, economic status, life experiences, political affiliation, so that the only difference between these two groups would be that of cultural similarity between the marital partners. Under these circumstances if one group developed a higher divorce rate, say, one would safely presume that cultural factors were significant in the differing divorce rates. Another approach would be to experimentally subject two groups to a stressful situation and note whether the two groups differed in response to the stress.

While ideal conditions of perfectly matched groups are probably impossible to achieve, it is worthwhile to look for conditions that approximate the ideal. One such group, the focus of study in this chapter, is the population of couples where one member suffers from chronic irreversible renal failure and is thus dependent on hemodialysis, the artificial kidney machine, for life. The onset of kidney failure represents a major stress on not only the patient, but also the spouse. This is particularly the case when hemodialysis is performed at home by the spouse together with the patient. In considering groups of homocultural and intercultural couples subjected to the onset of renal failure in one member of the couple and the need for home hemodialysis, one might hypothesize a number of outcomes: (1) If homocultural marriages are fundamentally stronger, then they should adapt more readily to the stress of a chronic illness and perform home dialysis more successfully. According to this hypothesis, intercultural marriages are already stressful and the addition of a chronic illness compounds the stress. (2) Another possibility is that intercultural marriages would more readily adapt to the stress and perform home dialysis better. One could hypothesize that an intercultural marriage requires stronger bonds and therefore would tolerate an external stress more readily. (3) Another possibility is that no difference would be found between the homocultural and intercultural groups. This would be expected if cultural similarity is an insignificant factor in couples' response to stress. This chapter reports a study of home hemodialysis couples which supports the second hypothesis above.

Hemodialysis as a Major Stress

Maintenance hemodialysis has been available for the treatment of chronic renal failure since 1960. In 1973, the federal government undertook financing the cost of hemodialysis under the Medicare program. This has led to hemodialysis being available to most patients who need it. The hemodialysis or artificial kidney machine is a large, formidable-looking piece of equipment through which the patient's blood circulates. Toxic waste products are filtered from the blood and the blood is returned to the body of the patient. Frequently the patient has an artery and a vein in one of his arms surgically adapted for easy access. For most patients, hemodialysis is done three times a week for about five to six hours each time. The machine as well as the patient's blood pressure must both be monitored throughout this period. In between dialysis procedures, the patient must take a number of medications and must follow a diet. Usually, this involves fluid and potassium restrictions.

Undergoing maintenance hemodialysis has been compared to a full-time job in relation to time and energy required, and patients vary greatly in their ability to adapt. A variety of psychological reactions commonly occur in response to this major stress. Emotional conflicts are often related to the dependency of the patient on the hemodialysis machine and on the hemodialysis staff. One form of maintenance hemodialysis, home hemodialysis, has been promoted to have major advantages for the patient. It is far less expensive, costing about $5,000 to $6,000 per year, compared to five times that for hospital-based hemodialysis. Home hemodialysis also offers the patient advantages in terms of time and mobility. Dialysis can be scheduled to his convenience; he need not worry about transportation to a hemodialysis center.

Home hemodialysis requires a partner to help monitor the machine. Both the patient and his partner have to be home trained until they are capable of running the hemodialysis and taking care of the variety of complications that might occur. Thus, for the partner, home hemodialysis involves taking on major responsibility, having less mobility and less free time. Most frequently, the partner is a patient's spouse. In these cases home hemodialysis presents a major stress to the marital relationship. During the home training period and during maintenance dialysis at home afterward, the couple must work closely together, knowing that the patient's life depends on their ability to do their duties correctly. Couples have widely differing styles of working together during home hemodialysis. Typically, the patient and spouse relate to each other in a manner characteristic of their style of relating prior to the onset of kidney disease. They attempt to adapt their patterns of relating to the problem of home hemodialysis. For some couples this works easily and smoothly. For others there are significant difficulties and for some the strain is too much and they are unable to continue home dialysis. For a few couples, divorce has resulted from the changes in their relationship required by home hemodialysis.

The setting of home hemodialysis provides an excellent backdrop with which to compare intercultural and homocultural marriages. Home hemodialysis is a significant outside stress, must be dealt with in the marital relationship, and cannot be dealt with by either partner alone.

It appears safe to assume that chronic renal failure will occur randomly to patients who have intercultural or homocultural marriages. All other factors being equal, comparing the adaptation to home hemodialysis of homocultural couples to that of intercultural couples should provide information about the strength of those marriages under stress.

Description of the Method of Study

The population selected consists of fifty-six couples, all of whom completed home hemodialysis training at least six months prior to this study at one large hemodialysis institute. Data regarding these fifty-six couples were obtained by reviewing medical records, social service summaries and also interviewing nursing staff who knew the couples. Data collected included ethnic group of both the patient and spouse, age of the patient, economic status, style of marital interaction including such parameters as dominance and dependence, and success or failure of the home hemodialysis. Success of home hemodialysis was defined as the patient being maintained at home for a minimum of six months until the time of the study, unless interrupted by transplant or death. Failures included those who could not be maintained for six months at home or those who eventually had to return to a hospital-based dialysis program.

Findings and Case Examples

Of the fifty-six couples who were home trained, forty-five were considered successful and eleven were failures. The ethnic group of both the patient and the spouse was known for fifty-one of the couples. Of these, thirty-seven were classed as homocultural and fourteen as intercultural. Table 1 presents the breakdown of the intercultural marriages. Of the thirty-seven homocultural couples, twenty-eight were successful at home hemodialysis and nine were failures (Table 2). Of the fourteen intercultural couples, there were no failures (Table 3). The probability that this difference could be explained by chance is less than 5 percent. There was no significant difference in age or economic status between the intercultural and homocultural groups. The proportion of male patients to female patients was very similar in the group of couples who succeeded and the group who failed. A few case vignettes are presented to convey the variety of responses couples have to home dialysis.

A female Filipino patient and her Japanese husband have a very close relationship. They have been at home for three years and feel that dialysis has brought their family closer together. Their two children are extremely helpful around the house, and the whole family treats the patient as someone very special. She likes to protest that she doesn't need all the attention.

A female Korean patient and her Caucasian husband have been successfully using dialysis at home for over four years. The patient throughout this period has maintained her job as a barmaid, something of which her husband does not approve. He tolerates this, however, and furthermore he adjusts his work schedule to fit her needs.

116

Table 1: Interethnic Home Hemodialysis Couples

	Patient		Spouse
Sex	Ethnic background*	Sex	Ethnic background*
M	Caucasian	F	Hawaiian
M	Filipino-Hawaiian	F	Portuguese
M	Portuguese	F	Japanese-local
F	Filipino	M	Caucasian
F	Filipino-Puerto Rican	M	Hawaiian
M	Hawaiian-Caucasian	F	Japanese
M	Chinese	F	Caucasian
F	Japanese	M	Hawaiian
F	Japanese	M	Filipino
F	Filipino	M	Japanese
F	Korean	M	Caucasian
F	Hawaiian	M	Japanese
F	Japanese	M	Filipino
F	Hawaiian	M	Caucasian

*Hawaiian includes part-Hawaiian.

Table 2: Homocultural Home Hemodialysis Couples

Ethnic background	No. of couples	No. of failures
Japanese	12	2
Caucasian	8	3
Hawaiian*	8	2
Filipino	6	1
Chinese	3	1
Total	37	9

*Includes part-Hawaiian.

Table 3: Success in Home Hemodialysis Related to Cultural Composition of Marriage

	Success	Failure
Intercultural	14	0
Homocultural	28	9

($X^2 = 4.133$, df = 1, $p < .05$)

A part-Hawaiian female patient and her Japanese husband have been on home dialysis for one and one-half years. The patient's family feels that the best thing she ever did was to marry a Japanese man. She is very dependent on him and he takes care of all her needs.

A Japanese female patient and her Filipino husband have been on home dialysis for six years. Her family does not approve of the marriage and they live with his parents. Both of them have full-time jobs, in addition to the hemodialysis. They get along with each other very well.

The following are examples of home dialysis failures.

A Japanese couple attempted home dialysis on two occasions, the first lasting three months and the second lasting only six months. Both the patient and her husband had a history of emotional difficulties. The couple would argue with each other during dialysis and even fight each other physically. They were unable to sustain a working relationship together.

A young part-Hawaiian female and her part-Hawaiian husband had a seemingly very good relationship. They sustained home dialysis for only ten months. The patient's parents disliked the husband and her mother was against the husband's performing the dialysis. During this period of pressure, the husband had an affair which led to a separation and the ending of home dialysis.

A middle-aged Chinese couple attempted home dialysis; however, they frequently fought with each other and at one point the patient refused to have his dialysis after a fight with his wife. Finally, an adult daughter took over the role of partner in home dialysis, since it was impossible for the patient and his wife to work together.

Discussion and Interpretation of Findings

While the intercultural couples clearly did better than homocultural couples in this study, caution must be exercised in interpreting the meaning of this difference. Since the present figures are based on what was found at one moment in time, many couples classified as successful still may end up failing at some point in the future. It is possible that this could happen to some of the intercultural couples. Another factor that does not show up in the study is that some patients had spouses potentially available to be the dialysis partner, but for one reason or another did not enter home training with them. There were two intercultural couples where the spouse chose not to be the home dialysis partner and home dialysis was accomplished with another family member. This also occurred for several of the homocultural couples. About midway through the period of this study, government financing eased the pressures on patients to choose home dialysis. This factor, of course, was the same for both intercultural and homocultural marriages.

A previous study of home dialysis couples noted that the pattern of marital interaction was significantly correlated with success or failure in home dialysis. Couples whose relationship was characterized by mutuality and reciprocity, a give-and-take relationship with each member responsive to each other's needs tended to do well in home dialysis. Likewise, couples where the patient was primarily dependent on the spouse partner also tended to do well. In these marriages the independent spouse would provide for and take care of the dependent partner's needs. For these couples, hemodialysis did not change the basic pattern of relating. The patient became increasingly dependent with his need for dialysis; however, the patient was used to depending on the independent spouse and this additional burden fit in naturally with the couple's usual patterns of relating. Independence in this context must be distinguished from dominance for it is possible to be quite dominant and yet dependent upon the partner for basic needs. The couples with the most difficulty with home dialysis were those where the patient tended to be independent and the spouse dependent in their relationship. In these relationships the spouse often had difficulty coping with new responsibilities of taking care of the patient.

An attempt was made to rate the couples in this study in terms of dependence, independence and mutuality. Ratings were done in an unsatisfactory way by means of putting together information from the patient's social history in the medical record and by interviewing nurses who had worked with the patients. From the data available, it appeared that among the homocultural couples eleven had relationships that could be characterized as mutual, thirteen had relationships characterized by the spouse being more independent and three could be characterized by the spouse being more dependent. Among the intercultural couples seven had relationships characterized as mutual, five were characterized as the spouse being independent, none were characterized by the spouse being dependent. Eight of the homocultural couples and two of the intercultural couples did not fit into these categories or not enough information was available. This data is highly suspect since eighteen spouses were rated as independent and only three dependent, whereas one would expect an approximately even split, there being no reason to believe that dependent partners in a marriage would be more likely to develop kidney failure. Nevertheless, there is no striking difference in the characterization of the marital relationships in the intercultural groups as compared to the homocultural groups, although the intercultural groups had a somewhat higher percentage of couples rated as mutual.

The evidence seems strong that intercultural couples react to the stress of home hemodialysis at least as well and probably better than homocultural couples in Hawaii. In speculating why this might be the case, it must be noted that intercultural marriages are commonplace and well accepted by society in Hawaii. Intercultural marriages are prevalent throughout the social strata of Hawaii. Another factor that must be taken into account is that the hemodialysis staff—doctors, nurses, and ancillary personnel—are multicultural themselves, reflecting the population of Hawaii. This staff is quite comfortable working with patients of all ethnic groups and seem to have no preconceived biases regarding intercultural marriages. Efforts are made to adapt the home training to suit the needs of the patient and his partner. This includes giving instructions in other languages when necessary. Special instructions and pictures have even been made to aid those unable to read. Thus, couples are not expected to behave only in set patterns, or fit a specific mold.

Families and relatives can play an important role in supporting or undermining a marriage. In the case examples presented there were supportive and nonsupportive families among the members of intercultural marriages. In other cases, the families were not living in Hawaii and not involved. There is no evidence to suggest that family support accounted for the greater success of intercultural couples, but it seems clear that family attitudes did not interfere with these couples' success in coping with the stress of home hemodialysis.

Looking at the results on another level, that of individual psychology, one finds the theory that intercultural marriages are based on neurotic needs to be highly suspect, since one would expect neurotically-based marriages to function poorly under stress. Indeed, the results support an opposing proposition, that an intercultural marital union tends to have stronger bonds and is more able to adapt to stressful circumstances than homocultural marriages.

Home hemodialysis is a specific and unusual kind of stress, and it could be argued that it is not fair to generalize from this situation to other stressful situations. To some degree this is probably true; however, because of the large adjustment in lifestyle necessitated by home dialysis and the strict requirement that the patient and spouse work closely together to make the adjustment, significant strengths in the marital relationship are almost essential for success at home dialysis. The impressive record of the intercultural couples performing home dialysis thus indicates that these marriages tend to be strong and enduring.

REFERENCES

Abram, H. S. Psychiatric reflections on dialysis. *Kidney International* 6:67-72, 1974.

Blagg, C. R., Hickman, R. O., Eschbach, J. W., et al. Home hemodialysis: Six years' experience. *New England Journal of Medicine* 283:1126-1131, 1970.

Smith, E. K. M., McDonald, S. J., Curtis, J. R., et al. Hemodialysis in the home: Problems and frustrations. *Lancet* 1:614-617, 1969.

Streltzer, J., Finkelstein, F., Feigenbaum, H., et al. The spouse's role in home hemodialysis. *Archives of General Psychiatry* 33:55-58, 1976.

12
Counseling for Intercultural Marriage

Jing Hsu, M.D.

Many studies have been carried out regarding the subject of intermarriage. Most of them have been focused on the frequency and divorce rate of intermarriage in different parts of the world and between different ethnic groups, and the backgrounds of persons involved in intermarriage, particularly regarding their age, sex, education, occupation, previous marital experience, immigrant status, motivation and adjustment, and so on. In general, it is widely accepted that difficulties are more likely to occur in intermarriages and that it takes more effort to make an intermarriage work. In spite of such information, however, little guidance has been given to partners in intercultural marriages and very few suggestions are available for the mental health professionals who are apt to be summoned to help when difficulties arise.

In this chapter, an effort will be made to outline the process of intermarriage counseling with particular emphasis on how to recognize the situations which may require professional counseling, how to assess patterns of interaction between intermarried couples, how to evaluate the potential areas of problems between them, and finally how to conduct therapeutic counseling for such intermarriage problems. Hopefully, this will generate more awareness as well as research in this particular area.

Intermarriage here is defined, broadly, as the mating of two individuals who may differ in religion, nationality, ethnicity, race, and cultural background. Generally there are five stages in which the married couple may seek professional help: premarital, marital, prenatal, preadoptive and parental. For the purpose of this chapter only the premarital and marital counseling will be discussed.

Premarital Counseling

A couple may come for counseling at their premarital stage if either they or their parents have some doubt as to whether the relationship will work. In general, the function of the counseling includes assessing the motivation for the relationship; discovering their expectations; finding the realities and helping the couple to see the differences, if any; forewarning about the difficulties that lie ahead; assessing the personal strengths of the couple as individuals and as a couple; assessing their compatibility; and finally watching for danger signals.

Assessment of Motivation. The primary function of premarital counseling is to assess the motivation for the relationship. There are several possible reasons for intercultural relationships, such as neurotic, emancipated, self-fulfilling, ideological and romantic motives, which are particularly in need of evaluation and concern. The following is a brief examination of these motives:

People who seek marriage as a solution to personal problems have a neurotic motivation. Neurotic motivations for marriage generally include escape from an unhappy home situation, revenge, rebound from a failed relationship, repudiation, material gain, status gain and so on. The same is true with intermarriage. For example, a German girl gets married to an American serviceman to escape the postwar poverty of Germany; a black writer marries a Caucasian to "get even" for every racial insult he has endured by taking her to bed; a woman who is rejected by her white lover may turn to blacks so she can feel like a "white queen" among them.

Unfortunately, neurotic marriages create more problems than they solve. Therefore, it is the counselor's primary function to assess the underlying motivation of the couple. If the counselor suspects that they are neurotic, it is his responsibility to advise them and help the couple postpone an immediate action until more discussion can take place and better understanding can be achieved. Long-term psychotherapy may be suggested if necessary. "When in doubt, defer; when still in doubt, refer."

Sometimes a couple's attempt to intermarry is not based on neurotic motivation, but is a result of weakened cultural identification and commitment toward the in-group, and traditional values may no longer have meaning to them. This is particularly true with young college students whose physical mobility not only prevents them from becoming deeply committed to their in-group culture and values, but also enables them to be exposed to different cultures and values. Their mates, while different in background, tend to have similar goals and personalities. It is safe to assume that this group would be more likely to have a better adjustment in intermarriage.

It has been postulated that there exist four universal human needs: namely, recognition, response, security, and new experience. Marriage to a person from a different background may be an attempt to meet the last need. It is exciting to fall in love with someone whose foreign extraction stimulates the imagination. The erroneous beliefs about the wisdom of the Orient, the sexual superiority of the black, and the wealth and opportunity of the American may pose great attractions to people who believe these sterotypes. However, good adjustment in marriage takes more than a breath of fresh air and a taste of foreign delicacies. The counselor needs to assess whether there is a basic personality compatibility which can hold the pair together when excitement and curiosity fade away.

With the growing feeling that people should be free to make their own choices, and with social revolution in progress, sometimes marriage to a particular individual is confused with dedication to a cause involving a group. This is particularly true with black-Caucasian marriages. Some people make intermarriage a test of their racial acceptance—"My greatest contribution to racial equality is to marry a Black." Entering a marriage to prove something is unrelated to factors which contribute to marital success. It should be pointed out that intermarriage, like any other marriage, should be entered into because two people want to marry each other regardless of their race, ethnicity, or religion.

A girl came into counseling under the recommendation of her father because he felt that his wife, the girl's mother, was facing a nervous breakdown as a result of the girl's relationship with a black boy. After a few interviews, the girl said that she had not realized before the implications and consequences of intermarriage, such as limiting her living to a certain area, giving up her Caucasian friends, and so on. She decided to go to New York and live in Harlem for a period to see what life in a black environment would be like if she would have to live in one. A few weeks after she had carried out her plan, she decided that the experience was too much for her and that she did not possess the pioneering spirit which such a marriage required. She was resentful of society imposing restrictions and handicaps on people simply because of the color of their skin, but she wondered whether the best way of fighting this discrimination was by flying in the face of society.

Most of the time, two people want to marry simply because they are in love, they feel irresistibly attracted to each other, or they believe that their life will not be happy or fulfilling without the company of the other and nothing else seems to matter at the time. They either ignore the cultural differences or are ignorant of the differences. People in love tend to spend most of their time alone together, so that they are relatively isolated from the world around them. Although love can exist in isolation and be enjoyed by itself, marriage cannot. The attitudes of family, friends, and members of society at large seep into a marriage; they cannot be completely walled out and disregarded. One of the criteria for success or failure in marriage is the degree to which a given marriage facilitates the removal or erection of barriers between the two partners and other people. The intermarried couple may find that they have difficulty in finding friends or that their families are not prepared to accept their spouses. The counselor should encourage the couple to get to know each other's culture as much as possible, by going through literature, by associating with the other's family, relatives, and friends, and thus getting a feeling of what the reality is like.

Evaluation of Expectations and Realities. Each culture or group has its stereotypical views of other cultures and groups, and individuals tend to project cultural stereotypes onto people of a culture without realizing that there are individual differences within the same culture or group. Therefore, they may relate to each other with preconceived ideas, prejudices and expectations. Intermarriage may be based on an illusion—what the partner should be like instead of what he or she is. The male-female role differentiation is an area which needs special emphasis. For example, a Japanese female enjoys the reputation of being submissive and obedient like an "Oriental doll." This may have been true in prewar Japan but hardly so with the current young Japanese generation. Therefore an American man who married a Japanese, looking for an Oriental doll, may find himself ending up with a "mother tiger," which is a Chinese nickname for a dominant and controlling wife. The problem becomes even worse if the Japanese wife married the American husband with the expectation that she would share equally in major decision-making.

The counselor can assess the gap between expectation and reality by posing specific questions for discussion. Areas that need special consideration are: the dissimilarity in attitudes toward women, their status, role, and the degree of restriction placed by custom upon their behavior; a woman's attitude toward her own position and toward men; attitudes toward authority; organization of the family with respect to relatives and in-laws; morality and aesthetics; and many other things. Henry Bowman, in his book *Marriage for the Moderns,* mentioned his counseling of an American college girl who fell in love with an Iranian. They planned to marry and live in Iran. In discussion, it soon became clear that there were several questions that she had never sought to answer, such as: Would the day-by-day existence as an Iranian wife be agreeable to her? What is the position of women in Iran? Would her relatives-in-law accept her and could she learn the language quickly enough to prevent the beginning of an unbridgeable gap between herself and her husband's people? Would she be satisfied to see her children reared as Iranians? Would the Iranian standard of living be acceptable to her? Are there any prejudices in Iran toward Americans? She did not know the answers to these and similar questions. The more she thought about it, the more she realized that there was little in favor of her plan and much against it. Therefore, she decided to break her engagement.

The counselor can also help a couple to bridge the gap between expectation and reality by encouraging them to read more about each other's culture and to associate more with one another's family, relatives and friends; or the counselor can present some common, real life issues for the couple to discuss and decide on as a way to experience life together. A run-down of actual wedding plans, living arrangements, religious and social activities may sometimes shed light on potential problems. For example, an American in Taiwan who had planned to marry a Chinese girl found out that while he was excited, imagining a traditional Chinese wedding, his Chinese fiancee was dreaming of a typical Western-style wedding.

Anticipation of difficulties. The counselor, based on his or her expertise in this area, is obliged to forewarn the couple of the possible difficulties that lie ahead for marriage in general and especially for intermarriage. The common sources of conflict between husband and wife are money, children, recreation, personality, and in-laws. In each of the specific areas, the difference in cultural background needs to be brought up for discussion and hopefully a full mutual understanding can be achieved before the marriage takes place.

There are additional difficulties for intermarried couples, such as the difficulty in finding housing because of racial prejudice, social isolation, rejection by the family, or homesickness. The coming of children poses additional difficulties: racial prejudice which was deeply buried may suddenly surface, for example, a Caucasian husband who can accept his Chinese wife may not be able to tolerate seeing his child with "slim eyes;" religious affiliation which has been in the background may begin to show strong roots in terms of child rearing, letting a child have his own choices is more easily said than done; differences concerning the raising of children become apparent and cause new problems and conflict; one or both of the spouses' families, who seemed to have been forgotten, may now be missed because pregnancy and childbirth bring back remote memories and revive early emotional attachments. All of these difficulties need to be pointed out to the couple and discussed.

Assessment of strength and compatibility. Although all marriages are bound to encounter various difficulties, intermarriage represents additional sources of conflict that will add to these difficulties. The counselor needs to assess whether the persons involved have the mental capacity or ego strength to handle such complicated situations, both as individuals and as a couple.

Individual strength can be assessed by past adjustment, educational and work history, interpersonal relationships, and coping mechanisms. To assess the relationship as a couple, inquiry can be made in terms of how the couple handles differences: Are they able to reach a compromise which is comfortable to both or does one always give in and resent it? How often and how intensely does the couple quarrel? Does quarreling result in better understanding and more acceptance or does it result in blocking off certain touchy issues that are no longer discussed? Do they respect each other in areas such as moral standards, habits, vocational choice, goals in life, ideals or judgment? Do they feel supported, valued, and appreciated for what they are? Do they feel that their relationship brings out the best in each other? Can they be happy in this relationship without strain?

It has been jokingly asserted that race, politics, religion, and sexual appetite are not at the heart and soul of a good marriage because what really counts is the divergence of tastes in matters such as garlic in food, bedroom temperature, and whether one of the pair is an inordinately early riser. Little things make or break even intermarriages. The great philosophical and social questions seem to take second place to these petty and practical concerns of daily living. A careful look at the compatibility of the couple in their family pattern and lifestyles would help to assess whether there is long lasting factor which will keep the two people together in spite of their major difference in background.

In many relationships, there are elements which indicate serious incompatibility between the two people. Such elements are danger signals which should be recognized early and the couple should be warned against trying to form a permanent relationship with each other. Judson and Mary Landis, in their book *Building a Successful Marriage* mentioned the following danger signals in marriage: repeated quarreling with a discernible pattern, repeated break-ups, a strong desire to change the other, feelings of depression and moodiness during the courtship, and a feeling of regression rather than of growing up.

The above mentioned danger signals can also be applied to intermarriage and should be watched for. Sometimes an extreme effort to defend a partner's race, religion, or culture also indicates a problem. This may well be a "reaction formation" to cover up one's deep-seated prejudice toward a partner's race, religion, or culture. One way of assessing one's prejudices is to learn to be aware of the responses to certain occurrences. For example, in an unpleasant encounter, one partner's race, nationality, or religion may come to the other's mind. If this is so, it is a clear indication of an intellectual commitment to be nonprejudiced and a lack of the intellectual-emotional ability to follow through.

Marital Counseling

When a marital problem occurs for the intermarried couple, there are two patterns to be observed regarding how they visualize the cultural aspects of their marital adjustments. One extreme is to blame everything on the cultural differences and the other is to ignore them. Of course there is a wide range between these two extremes.

During the different stages of marital life, a couple is bound to run into different kinds of problems or conflicts. A couple can either work together to find out how a problem came about and try to solve it, or they can blame each other. With intermarried couples, differences in cultural background, race, nationality, or religion often receive the blame for whatever goes wrong. Hugo Beigel described such an example: a black-Caucasian couple were worried about their sixteen-year-old son who was grouchy, hostile, shy, and withdrawn. The parents felt that his negroid appearance may have been responsible for his behavior. Beigel felt that the symptoms did not differ from the not-so-unusual phenomenon of adolescent troubles and rebellion, yet despite their otherwise well functioning marriage, the parents blamed themselves.

An even more serious problem occurs when cultural or racial issues are used as a weapon to attack a partner. In their article "Adjustment of Interethnic Marriage on the Isthnus of Panama," John Biesanz and Luke Smith said that happy as well as unhappy wives tend to attribute their happiness or unhappiness to the fact that their husbands are American and their husbands attribute the same with respect to their Panamanian wives. One American said that his wife was neat, another complained that his wife was slovenly, both said that "Panamians are like that." The peculiar thing about many intermarried couples is that they are alert and ready to make all of their discussions relate in some way or another to the racial angle. The black spouse finds it both an easy and a devastating weapon to condemn his white wife as not only white but also antiblack. The equation becomes "to disagree with me is to hate my race."

The counselor should first assess whether the problem is related to intermarriage. If it is not, then he should point out to the couple that their problem is not different from other couples', that intermarried or not, they should work together to solve the problem and stop blaming or attacking each other. Sometimes the counselor may find that the problem or conflict is indeed related to the difference in background. However, difference in background, such as race, is not something one can change; therefore the counselor should help the couple focus their discussion on something they can change, such as family patterns and lifestyles. For example, a Chinese husband and an American wife may quarrel with each other about their methods of disciplining their children. Nothing would be accomplished if each accused the other of being a poor parent because of cultural and ethnic background. If the discussion can focus on disciplinary patterns, then it may become clear that the father, as a Chinese, tends to be strict and that the mother, as an American, tends to be permissive, and then the two can work together to reach a disciplinary approach which will be acceptable to both. This approach not only prevents the couple from using difference in culture as an excuse or as a weapon, but it also provides new perspective and hope for the couple that life can be better and that they can do something about it.

The intermarried couple may ignore, deny, or even forget the discrepancies in their background and interpret the spouse's behavior to be based, in a way, entirely on the projection of his or her own experiences. Sometimes the culturally related or determined behaviors are taken personally and reacted to accordingly, thus creating misunderstanding and conflicts. The role of the counselor is to direct the discussion in such a way that the couple will be able to acknowledge the cultural influence in one another's behavior, and then look at the problem more objectively and less emotionally.

For example, a wife from Hong Kong became very angry at her Western-raised Chinese husband because she said that he was being unkind to her sixteen year-old son. Her husband did not want to give the boy any allowance or buy him a car to drive to school. The wife did not realize that the husband's cultural background was responsible for his believing that the child should not receive an allowance without working for it, and that a car for the son alone would be too luxurious. Thus, he was not really being unkind, but simply holding a different view of the matter as determined by his culture. The counselor should attempt to help the couple see the reasons behind the views of each person in this conflict and to realize that the conflict itself is not so much a personal one as it is culturally based.

In another example of cross-cultural misunderstanding, an American husband and a Chinese wife were newly married. The wife's father was going to have his sixtieth birthday, and the wife asked her husband for the money to return to her home country to celebrate her father's birthday. The husband was very unhappy and displeased by her request. He felt that they were not financially secure, referring to their mortgage and other monthly payments. He suggested that she simply send a card to her father. The wife became very upset and accused her husband of not loving her. She said that she would lose face as a daughter if she did not attend the birthday celebration, and she then attempted suicide. In counseling, this couple should be helped to understand why it is so important for her to go to her father's birthday celebration and why she feels obligated to do so, even though it is so expensive. The husband still felt that she was too attached to her parents and homeland. The counselor should help the couple understand that the conflict here is not so much a personal conflict as it is a cultural one, and help them feel less anger toward each other when they realize the different meanings that their cultures attach to the father's birthday.

Special Aspects of Intermarriage Counseling

When counseling an individual, it is vital for the counselor to maintain a neutral, objective, and "third-party" position throughout the process; this attitude is even more important and difficult to maintain in the so-called "couple counseling" situation. Although the counselor may be aware of the potential problems involved, and may try to maintain a neutral position, either one or both partners may attempt to persuade the counselor to take sides. In addition, the counselor may unconsciously identify with one partner on the basis of sex, age, similar personality or background.

In intermarriage counseling, the cultural, ethnic, or racial backgrounds of the counselor and of the couple become important because they are immediately visible and can be quickly identified and utilized by any of the participants. As a result, the counselor may easily form an alliance with one partner and may be accused of being prejudiced against the other, making counseling very difficult. Therefore, at the beginning of counseling, this issue should be brought into the open and clarified. The counselor should emphasize his desire to remain neutral and his wish that both partners call it to his attention if they feel that he is not doing so at any time. Without such a discussion, one partner may blame the counselor without real cause and use this as an excuse for not continuing or cooperating with counseling.

For example, a Caucasian wife and a black husband involved in a marital conflict came for counseling, at the wife's suggestion. The counselor happened to be Caucasian. When the sessions began, the husband expressed his distrust of the counselor and his suspicion that he would take the wife's side and that no one would be helped but the wife. The racial issue was significant even before therapy began, and resistance to any possible progress had been established because of past attitudes and experiences.

In another instance involving a Caucasian husband and an Oriental wife, the husband expected his wife to learn how to drive a car so that she would be able to do her own shopping, but the wife refused to do so. The husband felt that his wife was inadequate and not functioning socially as a wife should. The counselor, being Caucasian, had considerable difficulty in seeing the problems from the wife's point of view, that it was quite unusual for an Oriental woman to drive, and he tended to sympathize with the husband, based on his own background and expectations for a wife.

One solution to the problem of the counselor's possible cultural, ethnic, or racial bias or the intermarried partners' suspicion of such prejudice, involves the use of a counselor team, or cocounselors, each of a different background. Another possible solution is to utilize a counselor of a completely different background than that of either of the clients, so that no conclusions can be drawn prematurely. However, neither solution is optimal.

The possible gap in value systems. The process of psychotherapy or counseling can be defined as a process in which the counselor makes use of all appropriate strategies to help his client change his behavior pattern from "unhealthy" to "healthy." The concept of healthy versus unhealthy is, of course, not absolute. It is relative and subject to the sociocultural setting, thus becoming a very important issue in intercultural counseling when the counselor's background is different from that of his client's. This issue is further complicated in the intermarriage situation. Within such a counselor-client relationship, the three cultural orientations, that of the therapist and the two partners, must be considered in addition to the complicating factors of personality, sex, or life experience.

It is vitally important that the counselor constantly check his judgments and his own orientation which are products of his own background and culture. He must be careful in making suggestions, and he must constantly question these suggestions in light of his personal versus his professional judgment. It is particularly important that such judgments be made with a realization of the setting in which the couple lives.

Several specific issues which often arise in intermarriage counseling may involve value judgments based on cultural customs, taboos, or obligations. These include ways of spending money, divorce, adoption, extramarital relationships, and family relations, such as the obligations to in-laws. In such cases, the therapist should help the clients to see the possible alternatives in a problem situation so that they are not trapped in one cultural system, and to find the one best solution for them, both as a couple, and as individuals. The solution which is found should also be acceptable within the sociocultural environment in which they live.

The counselor-client relationship. The process of counseling and the counselor-client relationship differ with the culture in which it takes place. For example, a client from a traditional and authority-oriented background who seeks counseling may expect the counselor to be very "wise" and to know an answer to his problem and to give concrete and clear advice—whether he ultimately takes it or not. However, a client from another ethnic background may expect a more "equal" relationship and tends to discourage the inferior-superior roles; he may want a more cooperative, working relationship with his counselor.

The sex of the counselor may also affect this relationship because of the cultural differences in the male-female role. Some men may feel awkward and embarassed by bringing their problems to a female counselor because they expect the counselor to be authoritative and wise, yet in their culture, a woman is seen as otherwise. There are also many husbands who do not feel comfortable coming to a counselor to work out marital problems. The man in certain cultures may think that his private marital problems should not be discussed with outsiders; since a husband is supposed to be strong, he may feel disgraced by an admission that he cannot "handle" his wife. This type of husband-client perspective may be particularly resistant and negative toward therapy.

All the issues described are very important to the success of intermarriage counseling. In addition to the fundamental knowledge and skill required for regular marriage counseling, the counselor is advised to be sensitive to the cultural elements of intermarriage, to be aware of the cultural backgrounds of the partners involved in counseling, and to examine and handle the cultural aspect of counseling practice throughout the whole process so that a culturally relevant approach can be achieved. Indeed, intermarriage is a unique and complicated practice which is in need of more exploration, training and experience.

REFERENCES

Adams, B. N. *The American Family.* Chicago: Markham Publishing Company, 1971.

Adams, P. L. Counseling with interracial couples and their children in the South. *Interracial Marriage: Expectation and Realities.* Edited by I. R. Stuart and L. E. Abt. New York: Grossman Publishers, 1973.

Beigel, H. Marital and premarital counseling with interracial couples.*Marital Counseling.* Edited by H. L. Silverman. Springfield: Charles C. Thomas, 1967.

Biesanz, J. and Smith, L. M. Adjustment of interethnic marriages on the Isthmus of Panama. *The Blending American.* Edited by M. Barron. Chicago: Quadrangle Books, 1972.

Bowman, H. A. *Marriage for the Moderns,* 7th edition, New York: McGraw-Hill Book Co., 1974.

Day, B. *Sexual Life Between Blacks and Whites.* New York: World Publishing, 1972.

Klemer, R. R. *Marriage and Family Relationships.* New York: Harper and Row, 1970.

Landis, J. T. and Landis, M. G. *Building a Successful Marriage.*6th ed. Englewood Cliffs, New Jersey: Prentice-Hall, 1973

Lantz, H. R. *Marriage: An Examination of the Man-Woman Relationship.* New York: John Wiley & Sons, 1969.

Mudd, E. and Goodwin, H. Counseling couples in conflicted marriages.*The Psychotherapies of Marital Disharmony.* Edited by B. Greene.New York: The Free Press, 1965.

Otto, H. A. Premarital counseling. In *Counseling in Marital and Sexual Problems.* Edited by R. H. Klemer. Baltimore: The Williams and Wilkins Co.

Sanua: V. D. Intermarriage and psychological adjustment. In *Marital Counseling.* Edited by H. L. Silverman. Springfield, Illinois: Charles C. Thomas, 1967.